THE
SUPERMARKET
TRAP

DRAWINGS BY HELEN FULKERSON

Jennifer Cross

THE SUPERMARKET TRAP

The
Consumer
and the
Food
Industry

INDIANA UNIVERSITY PRESS
Bloomington & London

Contents

Appendices

Preface

This book was written primarily to tell consumers more about food industry operations at a time when food prices are rising sharply and housewives are anxious to know whether they are getting full value for money.

The need for more information became noticeable during the housewives' boycotts in 1966 and 1969. The food industry owed shoppers a satisfactory account of where their money was going and what changes were taking place behind the scenes. But it was never forthcoming. The boycotts generated a lot of mutual recrimination and protestations of innocence; the businessman's normal, deep-rooted reluctance to be completely frank with the public did not change.

Technological progress has also widened the information gap. Many consumers are worried about the safety of their chemical-laden food. Still more are finding their shopping skills eroded by scientific marketing, clever packaging, and new types of processing. Who, after all, can pinch a cyclamate? Or divine the amount of meat in a prepared dinner? Again, the food industry has been less than enlightening.

This book is an attempt to answer questions about those aspects of the industry which the consumer most frequently encounters. It began as a step-by-step inquiry—and grew from there into a commonsense look at a part of our free enterprise economy which has brought us undreamed-of luxuries at an unexpectedly high price.

It focuses on the supermarket, that bewildering, enticing, craftily packaged trap that awaits every housewife during her weekly shopping expeditions, which all too often leave her numb, fatigued, and slightly poorer than she anticipated. The contest is not an equal one, largely because most people are unaware that the trap exists, and of the competitive conditions within the food industry that sprung it, the marketing techniques that bait it so cunningly, or the waste that is one by-product of all this effort. The stakes are not peanuts; they are nothing less than the way our nation spends its $76.05 billion retail food bill, the growing volume of non-essentials, and who shall most influence this spending, the industry or the consumers.

It is not intended as a personal attack or crusade. There are many industries more concentrated, more wasteful, less efficient, and less responsive to public opinion than the food industry. If there is any villain it is the bind into which corporations are forced by the pursuit of profit, and the routine manipulation of the consumer to achieve this end.

Most of the information has been obtained from industry and government sources. A good many of the conclusions, too, have at one time or another been drawn by industry members themselves. In one sense this book is a tape recorder, eavesdropping on industry at its most self-critical. I hope for this reason it will also interest students in many different disciplines, who will find here a critical approach, plus a good many facts and figures not normally found in marketing textbooks.

Notes are collected at the end of the book. Those with an asterisk are mostly factual tidbits for general reading. The others are references to source material, mainly for students, academicians, and food industry attorneys.

Finally, a confession. Despite my attempts to be objective, I have a bias—for the consumer. I believe in the ordinary person's right to be well informed, and to protect himself from exploitation. So heavily are the odds stacked against shoppers in today's marketplace, that the knowledgeable consumers assumed by classical economic theory have dwindled to a hard core dubbed by the ugly industry word "consumerists." If this book can help redress this unfair balance, even in a miniscule and transitory way, I shall be more than satisfied.

J. C.

Acknowledgments

My thanks for help, advice, and information are due to a large number of individuals, corporations, and government departments.

In particular I should like to mention the following: Dr. Robert D. Buzzell, Fr. Robert J. McEwen, S.J., Mrs. Helen E. Nelson, Dr. Mabel Newcomer, Dr. Richard Holton, Dr. Lee E. Preston, Dr. Leland J. Gordon, and Dr. Colston E. Warne; my friends at the Berkeley Consumers Co-op and the Association of California Consumers, particularly Judge George Brunn, Mrs. Eva Goodwin, Mrs. Mary Gullberg, Mrs. Kendra Mon, and Mr. Robert Neptune; Mrs. Susan Kayman, of the Hyde Park Consumers Cooperative (Chicago); Congressmen Lester Wolff and Neal Smith; California Assemblyman John Briggs; boycott leaders Mrs. Carolyn Blessinger, Mrs. Virginia Kadow, Mrs. Rose West, Mrs. D. Herreras, Mrs. Pat Broffman, Mrs. Barbara Collins, Mrs. Shirley Tindall, Mrs. Glen Shrader, Mrs. Dixie Thiel, Mrs. Marilyn Cummings, and Mrs. Janet Stilwell.

I am also grateful to many dedicated public officials, particularly at the Food and Drug Administration, the Federal Trade Commission, the Department of Agriculture, the Western Regional Research Laboratories (Albany, Cal.), and the Alameda County Weights and Measures Department; to Dr. Alvin Carpenter and Dr. Jerome Siebert of the University of California Extension Service; to Mr. Rodney Leonard, now with the Children's Foundation; and to patient librarians in Berkeley, San Francisco, and at the University of California. I owe particular thanks to Wallace F.

Janssen, FDA historian, for his invaluable insight into FDA operations.

On the industry side, I should especially like to thank Mr. Ken Holl, of *Supermarket News;* Mr. Russell Pearson, and other members of Safeway Stores Inc.; Mr. Timothy D. McEnroe, public relations counsel for the National Association of Food Chains; Mr. Paul Cifrino, Chm. of Supreme Markets, Dorchester, Mass., the Super Market Institute; and the games companies Herron-Kienzle Inc. (Mr. Richard A. Wyatt), Miller-Waltzer Associations Inc., the Plaza Group (Mr. Howard Brown), the Glendinning Co., and Games Supplier Co. (Mr. Woody Wilson). I am grateful to the trade press, particularly *Supermarket News, Progressive Grocer,* and *Supermarketing,* whose supply of facts and figures provided such bounteous material, and occasional ammunition, for my story.

Finally, I should like to thank my husband Ellis Gans for his love and encouragement, for his help with proofreading, and for putting up with so many piles of paper strewn around the house while this book was being written.

THE
SUPERMARKET
TRAP

ne

THE DAY THE CASH REGISTERS
RANG "NO SALE"

There is organized labor and organized management, but with the housewives, the chains are doing as they like when the consumer ought to be boss. It's time the housewives taught the supermarkets a lesson they won't ever forget.

MRS. MABEL PATTISON
Housewives for Lower Prices, Denver

A saccharine description of the consumer in our economy is trotted out by classical economists, admen, and the food industry, particularly when they think the public may be listening: "Not the exploiter and not the robber baron but the *consumer* is king today. And . . . because of his 'dollar ballots' the *consumer will continue to be king*. Every day he casts those ballots at the cash registers. Business has no choice but to discover what he wants and to serve his wishes, even his whims."[1]

However, the food industry was electrified as lip service became a harsh fact in 1966, when housewives all over the country boycotted and picketed food chains in an attempt to bring prices down. In effect, the shoppers of America said: "You tell us we're queen of the supermarket—and we're telling you 'no sale!' "

Few of the protesters were "professional consumers"—indeed, the consumer organizations tended to sit on the sidelines inhibited by too much knowledge, or, in the case of California, because the issue was too hot for labor-consumer members to handle.

The boycotters were a good cross section of ordinary shoppers, from the slums of Harlem to the rich suburbs of Van Nuys. Their protests began in Phoenix and Denver and spread like brushfire among discontented shoppers from coast to coast, leaving a trail of (mostly) short-lived groups. Their names ranged from sober sounding Housewives or Homemakers for Lower Prices, to ones with snappy acronyms like MILK, WOW, YELP, and HELP.

What made the ladies wrathful was the upswing in retail food prices, noticeable since June 1965, and which peaked in August–October 1966. For the first time in seven years, food prices ran 1.1 percent above other items in the consumer price index (CPI); by December 1966 they averaged 5.4 percent higher than during all of 1965. Despite industry propaganda, it was clear that food was becoming less and less of a bargain, especially for families on low or fixed incomes. Early in 1966 the *Wall Street Journal* and the food trade press noted mutterings of discontent as women tried to ease the strain on their food dollars by cutting down on butter, bacon, and expensive cuts of meat. When bread and milk prices went up a few cents during the summer their patience snapped.

Both the food industry and the labor unions blamed inflation for the unprecedented price increases. However, management singled out the high cost of labor, shrinking food surpluses caused by rising exports, and heavy military buying for the Vietnam war; while the unions blamed soaring rents and services, which had gone up 54 percent between 1950 and 1965 compared to a 22 percent increase in wages. Farmers blamed bad weather, crop shortages, government agricultural policy, and the price squeeze put on them by the giant food firms. In a way, everyone was right—but in the atmosphere of recrimination and special pleading it was hard to discover the true picture. (See Appendix 1.)

But there was little doubt, however, how everything got passed onto the housewife. A Federal Trade Commission inquiry into bread and milk prices, published in October 1966, showed that the farmer was getting 0.6¢ more for the ingredients in a 1 lb. loaf, and 2¢ more on a half-gallon of milk. Yet the housewife was paying 1.7¢–3.9¢ more for her bread and 3.9¢ extra for a half-gallon of milk. The difference was taken by the bakeries, milk processors, and retailers, who not only added the extra cost of the ingredients but adjusted their profits, which were calculated on the basis of the total cost—a practice the FTC called "pyramiding."

These particular price increases not only pinched the ladies' pockets, they hit at their instincts as homemakers, aggravating them in a way that the rising cost of other things, such as medical care, did not. Many women believed that the supermarket chains were growing fat at their expense*[2]—others blamed middlemen or government spending. Weak in economics, they could not swallow the harsh fact that businesses exist primarily to make a profit, and that rising costs, including the rising cost of everyone's profit in the production-distribution chain, will be passed along to the consumer.

In their anger, the women hit at the only available target—the supermarket chains—demanding lower prices, either on specific foods like bread and milk, or right across the board. They also demanded an end to stamps and games, which, as it happens, are the two most controversial items in the bag of food marketing tricks.

The chains reacted badly, in disbelief that the housewives were serious, and in fright, both at the loss of business, and at the awesome spectacle of women on the march. To give in meant more price competition, even the threat of price wars, and they normally did everything in their power to avoid them.

So, many tried to give the women the runaround, particularly in the early stages of the protests. *Supermarket News* admitted that "By and large the organized housewives were snubbed by the re-

---

* Notes appear at the end of book. An asterisk indicates interesting reading rather than just a citation.

● Kooks, hippies, agitators—or just the awesome spectacle of Middle America on the march? The housewives' boycotts gave the food industry a shock from which it has not yet fully recovered. They also illustrated the businessman's dilemma in dealing with the public: to tell the whole truth is to get found out.

tailers."[3] Mrs. Rose West, leader of the Denver Housewives for Lower Food Prices, was told at the outset by one local food man: "You won't get off your duffs long enough to do anything." The Denver chains were unwilling to send representatives to address their meetings, and would not give frank answers to their (pointed) questions. Tactlessly they compared women shoppers to a herd of sheep, who never balked at the price of food since they did not have to earn the money to buy it.

The press appeared to be in collusion with the chains, who were among their biggest advertisers. With a few exceptions, the protest movement was ignored until it became hot news. After that, the press and TV rushed in, not without some misrepresenting. Later the chains complained that the whole thing had been blown up out of all recognition.

There were, of course, exceptions to the general brush-off. Most of the trade press and food associations urged retailers to do a better job of explaining the facts of life. A handful actually did. A few stores advised the women to boycott products that were especially high priced, and even offered to tell them when a particular manufacturer was about to raise his prices. The president of Publix Markets, Tampa, Fla., opened his books to the local protest group to show that his net profit was running at only 0.68 percent of sales—though he spoiled this gesture by refusing to drop stamps and games, adding, "We are not going to . . . let a small group of misinformed housewives tell us how to run our business."

As the protests spread, the food industry's sense of public relations came to its rescue. In California, the State Grocers' Association formed a speakers' bureau and used radio, press, TV, and local talks to put its message across. In New York, the merchants formed a "flying caravan"; in Kansas, they used posters, in Minnesota, an information committee. The Grand Union chain held special employee orientation sessions to teach staff what to say to angry or curious customers. A few even tried the gimmick approach, like welcoming picketers with coffee and doughnuts.

By and large the message was the same, the old propaganda, but louder, and with feeling. "Don't blame us, we're not responsible. There is no fat in our operation. Our net profits are low, only 1.3 percent of sales*⁴—how can we cut prices? Blame inflation. Why not try picketing the White House?" Faced with the new threat to their business, the stamps and games firms also pepped up their public relations. They hollered their traditional message that stamps and games were paid for out of the retailers' advertising budget, and that their cost was not passed on because the stores made so much in extra sales.

But food prices did fall, at least temporarily, on some products, in almost every city that had had a boycott. By the end of the year, the national average price on the Bureau of Labor Statistics index had fallen from a high 115.6 to 114.8,*⁵ and there were more "specials," which brought real prices down still further.

Some supermarket games were dropped like hot potatoes. Many chains also ditched stamps, at least in some areas, and lowered prices, or occasionally offered customers the choice of stamps or their cash equivalent. During 1967, some of the stamps and games of course came back—but at least the industry was having a fresh look at their usefulness. Stores' advertising was quickly revamped to suit the new situation. Chains that dropped stamps and/or games, or did not have them anyway, trumpeted "Look Ma! No gimmicks!" Everywhere there was a new emphasis on low, low prices, sometimes amusingly done by comic-strip heroes calling themselves "Price-fighter" or "Superguy."

While the women picketed, and the grocers racked their brains as to how to confront them, both parties in the November 1966 elections made magnificent political hay, using the boycotts either to attack or defend the government's fiscal policy. At the White House, Esther Peterson, first of the President's Special Assistants for Consumer Affairs, was being put in an increasingly difficult position. Though she had little real power to help consumers, she stretched it to the limit to see how much support the administration would give her in an open confrontation with business interests.

Her reward for allying herself with the boycotters was an intensification of the personal and political attacks from business which had been directed at her for much of her three years on the job. It became evident that the administration would not support her, and she resigned early in 1967. The *Wall Street Journal*[6] wrote this "obituary": "When she came out for the supermarket boycotts to protest the high prices, the food industry yelped. When she testified in Congress in favor of Truth in Packaging legislation, the Grocery Manufacturers of America and the National Association of Food Chains trumpeted their anti-administration protests . . . insiders say she was forced out by the Presidential fear of losing business support."

By the end of 1966—with certain notable exceptions—the housewives' groups were falling apart. Many of the ladies found protesting a searing experience. They encountered public apathy, hostility from the food industry, personal quarrels which fragmented many of their organizations, lack of time and money—in fact, all the normal tribulations of any consumer group. Many grew discouraged at the impossibility of changing the system by getting the chains to pass the message about low prices back to the wholesalers and manufacturers, thus starting a kind of pyramiding in reverse. Gradually, food prices began to creep back, almost to pre-boycott levels.

What, if anything, had the protests achieved? They blocked what might have been a 4-5% price increase in 1967 (see Appendix 1) largely because the chains were afraid to pass on further increases. Price wars were more extensive than usual. Many more ads began featuring low prices; chains even began to become discount stores. Naturally, profits suffered. From December 1966 onwards, a substantial number of companies[7] reported poor results, due in part to the boycott. In short, they proved the power of the consumer veto, which classical economic theory stresses but organized consumers have come to doubt. Gratifyingly, it was a veto that could exercise influence out of all proportion to the number of participants.

Almost as great as the shock to the pocketbook was the shock to the food industry's morale. In the usual tradition of American business, rising costs had been passed along to the consumer without serious expectation that the consumer would go on strike. Though discontent with high prices had been reported since the spring, ad nauseam surveys of women shoppers showed they liked high quality produce, stamps, and games. Around the time of the boycotts, a new survey by the authoritative Burgoyne Index, one of the industry's main indices of customer opinion, confirmed that women preferred low prices—but the message was not digested until the women actually came pounding on the gate. Perhaps the image of the typical woman shopper which, like Pygmalion, the industry had created, then fallen in love with, was out of date, too.

Such was the opinion of marketing expert William C. Nigut, who for years had been urging the industry to modernize its view of women. The honest-to-God homemaker, he said, is not necessarily "young, lovely, radiantly happy, hip, intelligent, fluent, interesting, white, socially active, sceptical, sophisticated . . . the Goddess of the Marketplace."[8] Eleven million are in reality widowed or divorced; twice as many are over 44 as are under 35; millions are Negro; millions are poor; and millions are lonely, using the supermarket as a cheap substitute for the psychiatrist's couch.

Substituting one stereotype for another is not necessarily an improvement, but at least the food industry was shocked into making a more genuine attempt to meet women shoppers and find out what they really like. The summer of 1967 saw a number of new experiments in this direction; the most ambitious was the Consumer Dialogues held by National Association of Food Chains in ten cities around the country; they were repeated in 1968. Each of these consisted of a panel of a dozen housewives, randomly selected within certain age and income categories, who answered questions about themselves and their food shopping habits before a gathering of local retailers. As genuine dialogues they were phoney, since the women did all the answering and none of the asking, and were kept in ignorance about their audience until the end. However, they provided the NAFC with a mass of new information, much of it conflicting, including women's views on the controversial stamps and games.

While the industry genuinely tried a little harder to improve its communications, it was still unwilling to level with public discontent over rising prices. In May 1969 a fresh wave of boycotts broke out, mainly in New York, Florida, and Colorado. This time their target was meat, which soared 8 points on the CPI index between May and July, and especially beef, 20¢-30¢ a lb. more than the previous year.

The fault, dear ladies, lies not in sirloin prices but in your paychecks[9] quipped rancher-broadcaster Ed Collins (sixty-seven midwest radio stations get his "Good morning, feeders, and Hello, mom"). Cattlemen simply could not keep pace with all those prosperous, meat-hungry families, and their demand had outrun the supply. His implication—and here he spoke for the whole industry—was that consumers were in some way to blame. Certainly the *farmer* was not getting fat on the higher prices. To prove his point, Mr. Collins presented a steer to Mrs. Micky DeLorenzo, attractive leader of the New York FLP boycott group, to give her firsthand experience of the trials of raising cattle.

Mr. Collins' presentation was extremely unfair in shifting the responsibility for the higher prices to public demand. He neglected to mention that the supply of beef is equally conditioned by how much (or how little) cattlemen need to produce in order to make an adequate income. They could lower retail prices by feeding more cattle, but fear to do so since their profit would suffer more than the meatpacker or retailer. Since 1967 they have been urged by the American National Cattlemen's Association to *reduce* beef supplies by 5 percent.

For the same reason they are dog-in-the-mangerish about letting anyone else increase the meat supply by relaxing the stiff import quotas from such countries as Australia and New Zealand. The *Wall Street Journal* commented:[10] "White House aides are wondering if they can rescue the housewife from high beef prices by letting in more imports, but they fear a stampede of angry American cattlemen." In reply to the charge of Congressman Henry S. Reuss (D-Wis.) that "outrageously high prices" are being supported by the quota system, a member of the President's Council of Economic Advisers, Hendrik S. Houthakker, commented wryly that changing the system was "a political hot potato" because domestic cattlemen could round up "50 senators with a single phone call" to oppose the move.

At this particular time, the reason for the market imbalance was inadequate supply rather than increased demand. In January, the U.S. Department of Agriculture reported that 10 percent more cattle were being fed, and 6 percent more were due to be marketed than at the same time a year earlier. Since the anticipated cattle never turned up, it can be assumed that the Department goofed— not, incidentally, for the first time.

A second complication was what two maverick meat companies —who placed an ad in the *Newark Evening News*[11]—called "wild speculation in cattle futures on the commodity market." The Chicago Mercantile Exchange, (it and the Chicago Board of Trade are the country's two largest commodity exchanges) denied the charge. But over a thousand consumers who read the ad were anxious enough to write to Senator Clifford Case (R-N.J.) asking how investors with perhaps no more than $400 to cover the speculative purchase of a $13,000 carload of cattle could influence retail meat prices.

A further mystery, interestingly enough pointed out by a Los Angeles supermarket meat buyer,[12] was why "when beef goes up, all other items, poultry included, go up accordingly." Well, said the industry, as housewives switch from high priced beef they create shortages (and high prices) of franks, bologna, chicken, and other protein substitutes. But perhaps Ed Collins was nearer the mark when he said that supermarkets were merely climbing on the bandwagon. Having read an article in the *Wall Street Journal*[13] forecasting higher prices all around, they raised their markups by as much as 65 percent.

Both boycott episodes left many people with an uncomfortable suspicion that there was more to the "free market" than could be met by glib explanations about inflation, or supply and demand. They also left the housewives with a fine appreciation of the double bind every businessman finds himself in when talking to the public. A half-loaf story provokes the feeling he is hiding something—but to "tell all" is to get found out.

It is this dilemma, combined with rising prices and poor performance, which is turning increasing numbers of consumers into "consumerists." While most of the original boycott groups disintegrated, many of their members got smart. Their leaders, in particular, did a fair amount of homework on food industry operations and became increasingly critical of the cost of such items as advertising, promotion, and supermarket services.[14] With no formal organization, Mrs. Rose West and thousands of other Denver women watch the local food industry like hawks; as a result, prices have risen less and price competition is tougher there than in most other cities.

Others have actively joined the consumer movement. The Virginia Consumers Council, which started as a boycott group, is now statewide, and claims to represent 70,000 people. The St. Louis, Mo., group HELP made a controversial pricing survey which showed that supermarkets in low-income areas were overcharging the poor. HELP members gave evidence on this practice at the Better Business Bureau of St. Louis hearings, and the House Government Operations Committee hearings. (See Chap. 8.) Mrs. Micky DeLorenzo, founder of FLP, carried her fight for lower meat prices right to a special inquiry on the subject, begun in October 1969, by the Special Studies Subcommittee of the House Government Operations Committee.

Today there are a record 47 national, state, and local consumer organizations. They are all symptomatic of a new, healthy desire on the part of shoppers to be honestly informed and fairly served —in short, to redress some of the balance of power currently tipped in favor of the giant food corporations.

Two

THE RISE OF THE FOOD INDUSTRY GIANTS

When a few large firms dominate a field, they frequently forbear from competing actively by price: competition by advertising, sales promotion, and other selling efforts almost always increases.

NATIONAL COMMISSION ON FOOD MARKETING
Food From Farmer to Consumer, June 1966

Many of the $64,000 questions put by the boycotting housewives were answered by the National Commission on Food Marketing (NCFM). This agency had been appointed by Congress in 1964 to find out what changes were going on in the (now) $110 billion industry, the biggest in the U.S., particularly changes that might add to the weekly food bill.

In June 1966 the Commission produced a thorough, well documented study, consisting of a 203-page outline, backed up by ten substantial technical studies, unreadable by anyone without a good deal of spare time and/or a training in economics. The Commission found that the industry was basically efficient. But it also found a change in the balance of power and the nature of competition, a change which was caused by the rise of a number of large,

well-heeled, and aggressive food manufacturers and retail chains
—trends which had been noticeable ever since the 1920s.

Both in retailing and manufacturing, little firms have been falling like apples in Autumn. At the same time, the biggest companies
have been getting a disproportionate share of the market, of the
assets in their particular industry, and larger, steadier profits. (See
Appendix 2.)

Hardly any of these big companies grew to their present size
and power solely on the strength of their superior mousetrap.
Impelled by the businessman's universal desire for growth, they
began by buying up their rivals, in the so-called horizontal merger.
(See Appendix 2.) Then, as they became well established, they
looked in other directions for an outlet for spare cash, for an opportunity to spread the manufacturing risk, away from areas
where demand was limited and preferences fickle, and for instant
size without the growing pains. Most of the retailing giants began
doing some of their own food manufacturing (see Appendix 2),
and some also dabbled in department, drug, discount, and other
types of stores (see Appendix 3).

Manufacturers also expanded into farming to gain better control over their raw materials (see Appendix 2), and into different
processing fields to find new outlets for their products, by-products,
or spare capital. Some thereby became transformed into giant
conglomerates; Armour, for example, primarily known as a meat-
packer, now also makes dairy and poultry products, soap, household waxes and cleaners, chemicals, adhesives, agricultural chemicals, heavy industrial equipment, and pharmaceuticals.

There is no doubt that the industry has given us a variety, and
in many cases, a quality of food which is unequaled anywhere.
Also, food prices have gone up less than the general cost of living,
with the exception of 1948, 1950–53, 1966, and most of 1969.
Whether the industry is as efficient as it claims is a different
question. The contention that "food is a bargain" because it takes
up a declining percentage of disposable income ignores the fact

that as people become richer they spend less on food and more on durable goods, transportation, entertainment, and services. The relatively low retail prices of recent years have partly been achieved at the expense of the farmer, who is getting more money, but not a bigger share of the consumer food dollar than in 1939. The food industry is less able to pass on price increases than many others. Women shop for food often enough to have a good idea of prices, and either scream when they go up or switch to a cheaper product.

The efficiency has not been achieved without some blood and sweat—and a concealed price tag. One change the NCFM commented on is that the larger and more powerful corporations become, the less they like price competition. Rightly or wrongly industry believes that most people can now afford to turn up their noses at modest price cuts, though they do respond to good promotion, clever advertising, and new products.

Even more to the point, price competition is avoided because it can trigger destructive price wars. The housewife gets a lot of cheap food but the industry loses money, which is what happened to some food chains after the boycotts when they ditched promotions and slashed prices. Another reason is the delicate web of interconnections built up between the larger companies as they grew and merged; it makes business profitable and moderately gentlemanly, provided everyone sticks to the rules.

An example of what happens when a firm turns maverick is Consolidated Foods, a processor-become-conglomerate, which started a "miracle price" promotion in 1965 in its seven Chicago Eagle Food Centers. In retaliation, its big rival, the National Tea Co., with 237 stores in the area, boycotted an important Consolidated product, the baked goods from the Kitchens of Sara Lee. The squeeze lasted only one week, when Eagle Food's prices reverted to normal.

Small wonder that the giants prefer to compete through marketing, the modern corporation's tool for identifying broad areas of consumer interest, creating acceptable products, and manipulating demand to get optimum sales—in short, for that medium-long-range planning which is essential to their growth and security. Of course it adds to the cost of doing business, but is a form of gamesmanship where the resources of competitors and the rules of the game are well known.

The end result is the extravaganza many consumers complain of—stamps, games, and other promotions; more elaborate stores; heavier advertising; price juggling; the flood of new products; and the increased emphasis on packaging. Many of these things provide genuine value to the consumer, though whether they are as useful as price cutting, particularly to low-income people, is a debatable point. Unfortunately, along with upgraded stores, food that is more varied and convenient and better packaged goes an increasing amount of waste: advertising and promotions that stalemate, new products that flop, inflated and deceptive packaging, all of which are ultimately paid for by the consumer.

The demise of small businesses has not always been an un-mixed blessing either. Many of them simply lacked the money or management skills to keep up with changing times. But some medium-sized firms were bought up precisely because they were efficient, and could offer a good brand name or a big share of a local market. Sad to say, an unknown but probably substantial number were deliberately driven out of business. Cases before the Federal Trade Commission and the Justice Department in the last two decades show that some were hit by subsidized selling (sometimes below cost) by big chains as they broke into new markets and could afford to make up losses in a few areas by profits from others.[1]

In the bakery business many large companies used their financial resources to drive smaller rivals to the wall, a process aptly called "clobbering." In 1959, bakers testifying before the Senate Anti-trust and Monopoly Subcommittee hearings on administered prices in the bread industry described how it was done. Companies which could afford to give bread away to get a foothold in a new market would send trucks which "drove around town and

in adjacent areas all day, finally giving the bread away to insti-
tutions, putting it in people's cars, meeting people after work and
telling them to help themselves, and actually offering to supply
grocery stores with free bread for a considerable length of time."[2]

Another tactic, which was so common in the twenties and thirties
that it led to the Robinson-Patman amendments to the Clayton
Act, and which is still going on, is to give allowances for advertising, promotion, or quantity discounts to favored (large) customers
instead of making them equally available to all retailers.[3] From
1959 to 1965, 88 percent of the cases that came before the Federal
Trade Commission involved food firms: the manufacturers who
gave the allowances, and the retailers, generally large chains, who
received them, and in many cases, pressured for them. All nine
top chains of the period were implicated in this practice, most of
them more than once.*[4] Most of the more flagrant cases involved
dairy and bakery companies who were competing in local markets
for the patronage of a handful of large chains. The chains did half
or more of the business in the area, and already had or were likely
to start their own bread and milk processing.

When giant firms clash or move over small competitors into new
markets, the public does not always benefit. At first sight it would
seem that when a company gives bread away or temporarily lowers
its prices, the consumer wins. But lower prices in one area are always made up for somewhere else where the company has a strong
market share. Sometimes a whole city can be hit by this particular
game. In Washington, D.C., 1969 food prices were noticeably
higher than in other major cities. According to the FTC, this was
caused by the monopolistic pricing policies of four firms (Safeway,
Giant, Grand Union, and A & P), which hogged 60% of the total
market.

When the competition becomes killing, the companies sometimes try to fix prices, again particularly on bread and milk. For
example, Safeway and fifty bakers in the state of Washington con-
spired to fix bread prices from 1954 to 1964; they jacked up local
prices by 20 percent, and prices fell only when the FTC investigated.

As a result, consumers lost $35 million during the ten-year period. Had this been a national conspiracy, the public would have been bilked of $2.7 billion.

Aside from these dirty games, which were mainly a feature of their brash youth, there are signs that the giant food firms are reaching a stalemate. The economies resulting from the retailing revolution begun in the twenties and thirties have run their course. At that time, food chain prices were 6–14 percent lower than their competitors, and these low prices were permanent, unlike today's specials. They were achieved through combining the wholesale and retail function: chains, then later, affiliated independents, started their own warehouses and group buying arrangements. Then followed the self-service supermarket, which drastically lowered costs by sloughing off much of the work to the customer, who had to select and cart her own groceries, and to the manufacturer, who often delivered the goods, serviced the displays, and supplied free sales material, advertising, and promotional allowances.

After World War II, food retailing profits were high and grocery stores appeared everywhere, particularly in the burgeoning suburbs. Today chains and groups are increasingly competing against each other as small stores fall by the wayside. Allowing for differences in management and market share, the large stores are about equally efficient. All use similar retailing and distribution methods, and all find it increasingly harder to achieve new economies. Great strides are being made backstage; electronic data processing makes possible more efficient ordering and tighter inventory control, and mechanical handling speeds goods from warehouse to storage and onto supermarket shelves. But the actual selling function is difficult to automate. Like everyone else, stores find it hard to get good staff, and are now using slightly more part-time help than full-time, only to discover that two halves do not equal one whole. Also, with larger stores and vaster parking lots, total space is less efficiently used.[5]

Operating expenses have been rising, an inevitable trend in what economists call the "wheel of retailing." After stores reach the limit of price competition, they spend more on fancier premises and longer hours, and promotions like stamps, which cancel each other out. A steady rise in the number of items they carry has led to stocking and handling problems, and has had a dampening effect on turnover. Add the complication of unionization among clerks and butchers (which has resulted in fairer and higher wages) and inflation (which has raised the cost of everything), and it is not surprising that rising costs have been eating into profits for the last fifteen years. (See Appendix 4.)

Though now aware of these trends, supermarkets are unable to halt them. The capitalist system has no mechanism for knowing when it has reached an optimum level, thus businesses' pursuit of their short-term self interest always causes the system to go past this point, with more or less painful results. These might be avoided by industry cartels, or government regulation, except that the first are illegal and the second unpopular. Hence we are stuck with paying a high price for excessive competition.

A second industry trend is that agricultural products are becoming more costly. Between 1940 and 1964 the number of farms halved,[*6] yet output per man has gone up by 6.3 percent yearly, almost three times as much as the non-farm economy. In 1940 one farm worker produced enough to feed nine city dwellers. Today—thanks to automated planting, milking, harvesting, and picking; scientific breeding; and the increasing use of chemicals and pesticides—he can feed forty-five. Unfortunately the miracle has not helped the farmer gain a bigger share of the discretionary food dollar. In 1939 he got 39¢; in 1969 he got the same. He survives in the face of his increased expenses only because of his increased productivity.

The main reason for this cost-price squeeze is that farmers chronically grow more of a perishable product than can be consumed, and cannot wait for the right buyer or the fair price. Even organized in cooperatives, they have weaker bargaining power than the brokers, wholesalers, retailers, and processors who buy from them. They have also been somewhat browbeaten by the rise of the giant food firms. As the giants turn farmer—specifically, begin to own cattle and process meat, or enter the poultry and egg business—they present farmers with fewer but more powerful buyers. As fruit and vegetable processors, particularly canners and retail chains, start to do their own buying, they bypass the terminal markets which traditionally set the market price.

Farm prices jumped 7.3 percent in 1966, causing the increases in bread, milk, and other food which triggered the housewives' boycotts. In 1967 they fell 4.9 percent, only to rise 3.2 percent in 1968 and 4.9 percent in 1969. Meanwhile, many farmers were muttering that the government should keep its hands off agricultural prices and leave them to the free workings of the market. If this happens, the days of cheap food may be over for good.

Another very mixed blessing for the consumer is the food industry lobby. Though not as well organized as, say, the medical profession, it frequently clashes with the public interest. Mercifully this pressure group is not united, but consists of hundreds of separate organizations representing farmers, individual producers, manufacturers, canners, freezers, packagers, and different types of retailers, many of whom are at odds.

However, the industry is extremely strong in Washington. Strong enough for Ralph Nader to ask the House Government Operations Sub-committee to investigate what he described as a growing corporate crime wave.[7] Farm and agribusiness groups like the National Farmers Union and the American Farm Bureau Federation are among the top lobby spenders in the capital. Sixty-eight food and agriculture trade associations have Washington offices, and still more retain public relations and legal counsel there. The industry has close unofficial ties with the Department of Agriculture and the Food and Drug Administration. It is also politically strong in certain states, particularly California, where there are some seven hundred industry organizations, many of them extremely influential.

As a huge advertiser, the industry has considerable influence

over the national media. Fear of advertiser retaliation, though un-
founded, still lingers, particularly among the big magazines and
local newspapers.[8] There is also a strong reciprocal bond between
the media and their sponsors. Many national magazines do valuable survey work for the industry on women's shopping and eating habits. *Reader's Digest* has even contributed a number of short
movies, to be used by the industry for training or public relations
purposes.[9] In return the industry spews out free samples of new
foods, press releases, recipes, and nutrition news. It also hosts the
annual National Food Editors' Conference, and, in 1968, organized
a special series of dialogues in thirteen cities to warn members of
the press, radio, and TV of the possibilities of further price increases
and the need to turn away wrath.

The media may not be quite in the industry's pocket, but they
have certainly leaped to its aid in time of crisis, for example, over
Truth in Packaging. While the hearings were in progress, G. A.
Willis, then president of the Grocery Manufacturers of America,
breathed wordy but unmistakable warnings to remind a group of
sixteen top magazine publishers and the TV Bureau of Advertising
of the "interdependency" between them and "their bread and
butter." He hinted they should say something nice about the food
industry, fast. The result was articles in *Reader's Digest, American
Weekly, This Week, The Saturday Evening Post, Look, Life,
Ladies Home Journal,* and provincial papers all over the country,
stressing that food is a bargain. The proponents of Truth in Packaging were out in the cold. Three of Senator Philip A. Hart's
television appearances were inexplicably canceled, and a feud
started against him and Mrs. Esther Peterson by *Look* magazine.
The Metropolitan New York Consumer Council was refused an
appearance on the "Today" show to reply to Congresswoman
Catherine May, a Fair Packaging and Labeling Act opponent.
Even A. Q. Mowbray, author of a witty but critical book on the
subject, *The Thumb on the Scale or the Supermarket Shell Game,*
was hit by a press publicity blackout.

During the NCFM hearings, the Grocery Manufacturers of America persuaded its magazine and TV friends to pitch in $200,000 of the $400,000 raised to finance its own (more favorable) report on the food industry, and got six magazine editors to ask the Commission for a special hearing at which they put across the message of how satisfied consumers were with the industry. After the NCFM report was out, the Magazine Publishers Association moved in with a campaign for freedom of advertising and against grade labeling. (See "those Albania ads" in Chap. 3.)

Another result of this interdependence is the uncertainty with which the press, radio, and TV handle consumer issues, never their strong suit at the best of times. The Denver press was so slow to cover the start of the housewives' boycotts simply because they were not sure they were news. Weights and measures officials generally complain of poor coverage. Until very recently public discussion of consumer problems has been either conspicuously absent or biased—a situation for which business is responsible. It is a high price to pay for new product news and glossy ads of mouthwatering meals.

The packaging issue is not the only one in which the industry has taken a "public-be-damned" attitude. It also maintained a long, suspicious silence on meat inspection. When that failed, it supported the weakest version of the Meat Inspection Act, and attempted to amend the Poultry Products Inspection Act by weakening the USDA's power to walk straight in when the quality of state inspection started to waver.[10]

When the House Government Operations Committee report on supermarket operations in low-income areas was due to break, with its damaging allegations of price discrimination by the giants in some ghetto areas, food retailers tried to suppress or modify the report.[11] The attempt failed. However, when VISTA (Volunteers in Service to America) broadcast a TV spot accusing grocers of raising prices the day welfare checks were cashed, Clarence G. Adamy, President of the National Association of Food Chains, got it withdrawn by protesting to OEO, VISTA's parent agency.[12]

The industry has consistently balked at providing consumers

with certain basic shopping information. It has criticized the idea of grade labeling—quality grades which would tell shoppers what they wanted to know and which would be simpler to understand than the present chaotic system of USDA grades. (See Appendix 11.)

A few years ago, when the USDA developed consumer grades for thirteen popular vegetables and fruits, the industry's reaction was a mixture of hostility and massive indifference to a measure that at best would bring no profit, and at worst might damage their brand names. These grades would have been applied at the wholesale level and would have cost the trade money, since wholesalers, brokers, and shippers normally foot the bill for all voluntary grading. And since all of them were completely used to the old No. 1s, 2s, and Extra Fancys, they saw no reason to adopt a new system. In the wry words of one USDA official, "Perhaps some commodity people get a little ego involved and don't see any advantage in change." As a result, the new grades were never used.

On the grounds of keeping product secrets, the industry has also refused requests to list *all* the ingredients, and the percentages in which they appear, on *all* foods, not merely those for which there are no food standards, and the pathetically few cases (e.g., pet food and certain syrup blends) where the FDA managed to wring a decent contents statement. Since 1962 industry has opposed the FDA's attempt to draw up some regulation of special dietary foods and supplements, which would bring a little law and order into the jungle of low-calorie claims. Joining forces with the drug industry, the giants playfully bullied the FDA's consumer witnesses—a standard treatment, which nonetheless petrifies all but the stoutest heart. Attorneys earning $100–$200 an hour tied them up so thoroughly with legal gobbledegook that one home economist complained, "After four days of testimony, I hardly knew my own name."

Where food standards are concerned, the industry often uses the fillibuster technique, patently putting their concern for sales way ahead of quality, or even safety. The classic case, involving peanut butter, dragged on for ten years. Manufacturers had the temerity to suggest that consumers, particularly kids, actually *did not like* peanut butter containing 90 percent peanuts, the FDA minimum, and the millions of "Skippy" eaters satisfied with less could not be wrong. When the FDA proposed standards for specialty breads, which contain far less eggs or butter than consumers expect, the bakers' lobby fouled up the proceedings by slashing the FDA's modest minimum from 5 to 2 percent egg, and 12 to 4 percent butter. There is still no standard for these breads, which typically contain half an egg or ⅜ oz. of butter (each worth 2¢) but may cost twice as much as regular bread.

When the FDA proposed restricting the use of antibiotics to treat animal disease and promote growth (1968), meat producers claimed that their losses would more than outweigh the dangers to the public health. Yet the use of antibiotics has actually fostered bacteria strains that resist all treatment, while drug residues in meat can cause allergic reactions in humans. (See Chap. 9).

Still more recently, meat processors battled through half of 1969 to impose *their* version of a standard for the fat content of franks and other cooked meats. Already using these products as a dumping ground for unwanted fat and substandard meat, manufacturers were hostile to the prospect of *any* regulation. Faced with this ultimatum, they proposed a high limit of 33 percent fat (which the USDA meekly endorsed) vs. consumer groups' request for 25 to 26 percent. Somewhat to everyone's surprise, a compromise figure of 30 percent suggested by Mrs. Virginia Knauer, the President's Special Assistant for Consumer Affairs, was adopted—thanks largely to Mr. Nixon's well-publicized comment that he was on a low-cholesterol diet, and felt that 30 percent fat was quite sufficient.

The heavy hand of the profit motive can also be seen in many of the industry's dealings with weights and measures. Aside from the question of sharp practice, one section of the industry—the bakers—have obtained a sweet deal in ten states[13] by getting legislation passed which exempts them from producing an exact 1 lb. loaf. This has resulted in a 15–17 oz. standard loaf in some states,[14] and that bloated monstrosity, "balloon bread," a standard 1 lb. loaf which has been inflated with air to make it look bigger and baked in a 22½ oz. pan. There is no justification for this degree of tolerance, which amounts to 6.3 percent, and virtually legalizes a 1 oz. per pound shortage. The industry can just as well bake a 16–18 oz. loaf.

Even farmers, despite their current sympathy pitch to housewives over agricultural prices, have not necessarily directed their political influence towards the public good. The dairy industry engineered punitive legislation against the sale of margarine; the Federal Filled Milk Act, which prohibits the sale of filled milk*15 in interstate commerce; and legislation in thirty-two states preventing the production and sale of filled milk. At the same time, milk producers have worked their way into a neat monopoly. In the majority of states, wholesale milk prices are set according to the end use of the product, a device which has discriminated against milk for manufacturing purposes in favor of top grade fluid milk. Retail price setting in about half the states prevents big chains (who can afford to do so) from lowering prices. (See Appendix 1.) As a result of these two measures the public is paying more for its milk than if the market were free. Farming interests have a consistent record of opposing farm labor legislation, which has given them a bad name in the opinion of people liberal enough to believe in the principle of fair wages for a fair day's work.

Looking at these various issues, certain goals become apparent. The industry is against any measures which will cost money without yielding a profit. It is against government action, except in its own interest; government action on behalf of the consumer or labor is categorized as "interference." It also wants the maximum latitude over weights and measures and food standards; in short, over the rules by which business shall be conducted.

The food industry giants are not monsters. Their goals are shared by the majority of giants in other industries, for whom looking after "number one" is the first rule of commercial life. The only person this may possibly surprise is the housewife—not because she is naive, but because the industry may have succeeded in persuading her that *she* was number one.

Three

THE HIGH COST OF ADVERTISING

Probably half of every advertising appropriation is wasted, but nobody knows which half.

LORD LEVERHULME, 1851–1925
Chairman of Lever Bros.

During 1968 a curious series of advertisements that became known in consumer circles as "those Albania ads" appeared in a hundred magazines. Their message was that if the government started to tinker with the competitive system by limiting advertising or substituting grade labeling for brand names, we would all be back in the days of the Model T, when grandma had to slave eight hours to produce Thanksgiving dinner. There would be no variety, no fun, and we might as well be in Albania.

The ads, run by the Magazine Publishers Association, were typical of what passes for a dialogue between industry, economists, and social critics on the wastefulness of our competitive society, particularly as manifested by advertising—a dialogue which is more a series of monologues conducted in an angry whine, where critics complain that advertising is vulgar and wasteful, and its defenders reply with the Albania argument. Unfortunately such exchanges force both sides into extreme positions. The critics are reluctant to admit that some advertising is good and useful, and industry will not concede, as it does in private, that advertising also involves waste.

In this case, the "Albania ads" were prompted by the conclusion of the National Commission on Food Marketing that advertising might be responsible for some fat in the food bill. Between 1950 and 1964 food advertising quadrupled, increasing one-third more than advertising by all U.S. corporations. It was the most rapidly growing item in the whole marketing bill, which had gone up more than one-third during the same period.

The NCFM suggested that the industry's principal inefficiency was "the cost devoted to selling efforts that yield little value to consumers."[1] It added that "an unknown but substantial proportion of advertising and sales promotion serves only to urge consumers to patronize firm A instead of B, or buy brand C instead of D."[2] While accepting that the selling function could not be eliminated, "it might be substantially reduced without impairing the value of the final products to consumers."[3]

These fairly mild conclusions raise some highly pertinent questions. Exactly how much of the whole selling function, of which advertising is a part, fails to achieve results by industry criteria, and is of little or no benefit to the public? Where does such waste occur? Can it be reduced? And, since advertising and selling are the principal ways in which the giants compete, how effective is competition in the food industry?

A hard look at the industry leads to the inescapable conclusion that competition has gotten way out of hand. The process of every manufacturer pursuing his own maximum growth and profits has led to an overcrowded marketplace, where firms have to escalate their sales effort just to stay in business, let alone expand, and consumers are offered far more variety than they can cope with, both as individuals and in the aggregate.

There are simply too many products for people to buy. Since

1946 the number of items stocked by the typical supermarket has risen from 3,000 to 8,000. Nationwide there are nearly 35,000 different items available in the grocery and housewares sections, not counting meat, produce, or dairy products.[4] Each year brings more: 7,303 new items in 1966, 8,000 in 1967.[*5]

It would take more than a lifetime to sample the items in just one store, even if we had the time and inclination to make a thorough, rational choice. In practice, we can remember only 1,200 brand names (not all of which are foods) and to keep sane, must screen out more products than we would ever buy or even consider. Allowing for different tastes, the cumulative result of this screening is that some products are invisible on the shelves. They cannot penetrate the hypnotic trance in which so much of today's shopping is done. Hence they are not bought, regardless (up to a point) of how good and useful they are.

Supermarkets are also forced to screen products by sheer pressure on space. An A. C. Nielsen study[6] found that in one week a store accepted only 18 new products out of a total of 79, and that most of the "also rans" were rejected out of hand without getting as far as the buying committee. Even the ones that get this far are evaluated very haphazardly. All too often the product plays second fiddle to the size and reputation of the manufacturer, the quantity and type of the introductory advertising, and the sales allowance. There is an odd reluctance to consult store electronic data processing records to see how well similar products are selling.

Even manufacturers are forced to exercise a good deal of product "birth control." Only 4 percent of the brain children spawned by research and development ever get to full marketing.[7] Eighty-one percent never get farther than the idea stage; the rest fail during testing or test marketing.

As a result of all this screening, a large number of new products never make good. Industry figures imply that 80–95 percent will flunk; this figure varies from company to company among different types of products. A more detailed survey by Harvard professors

Robert D. Buzzell and Robert E. M. Nourse[8] found that 39 percent failed by the time they were in full distribution, and 40 percent of the remainder were only moderately successful.

Relatively few of the so-called "new" products that survive are really innovative. According to E. B. Weiss, a marketing expert and the industry's voice of doom in *Advertising Age,* "at least 80 percent of new products aren't new products at all. They are simply modifications—and minor modifications at that—of existing products."[9]

The word "new" had been abused to such an extent that Buzzell and Nourse had to divide it into three categories. "Innovative" products—the newest kind of new—were those that no other firm had ever produced before. "Distinctly new" products were those that were new enough that the manufacturer had to put in the basic work of research and development and test marketing. "Me-toos" were products that could be fitted into existing product lines with almost no cost and dislocation. These "me-too" products include housebrands, new packages, new sizes, new flavors, and manufacturers' duplications of existing products, new perhaps to the company but umpteenth in line on the shelves.

During their new product study (1946–64), Buzzell and Nourse found fewer than twenty items they felt were truly innovative: dehydrated (flaked) potatoes, all-purpose instant flour, frozen juice and synthetic juice concentrates, liquid diet foods, instant nonfat dry milk, precooked rice, semi-moist dog food, powdered non-dairy creamers, three types of cold breakfast cereal (presweetened, nutritional, and with dried fruit), soft margarine, freeze-dried soluble coffee, boil-in-the-bag vegetables, and frozen dinners. Since then, two others could be added: dry cocktail mixes and space food sticks.

Very few of these innovative products really set the house on fire. There is less difference between canned and semi-moist dog food than between manufactured dog food and table scraps. Soft margarine is only a small advance on the ordinary; so is minute rice vs. conventional, frozen concentrated orange juice vs. canned or fresh, non-dairy creamers vs. half-and-half. Their strong suit tends to be convenience, which is important to many people, but not necessarily higher quality. Some new products may also taste worse, from a gourmet point of view, especially the synthetics and non-dairy substitutes for the real thing.

In occasional bursts of honesty the industry admits the marginal nature of such offerings. For example, *Forbes Magazine*[10] explained the brand explosion among pet foods in human terms. People like their pets to eat as they do; they also switch brands in the hope of finding one their pet will prefer. Yet "the logical way to feed a dog is simply to buy an inexpensive 50 lb. bag of food and feed him the same every day. If the dog doesn't eat, say 'to hell with you' and offer him the same thing 24 hours later. Dogs don't need variety. That's a myth."

Marginal or not, the true cost of new products is much higher than people realize. "The development of a new product is much like a gigantic crap game. The stakes are extremely high, and the cost of failure, by not getting into the game at all or by launching unsuccessful products, is astronomically high."[11]

Every product in the "distinctly new" category that fails before achieving national distribution will set the manufacturer back an average of $342,000; if it fails after one year of full marketing the total bill will be $1,749,000. If the product is an innovative one (which is unlikely, because failures in this class are rare), it will cost $795,000 for introduction and $5,706,000 for one year's marketing. For the entire industry, the costs of flunking are at least $108 million a year—quite apart from the me-toos.

Manufacturers have to hustle to attract and hold strong distributors and dealers, merely to get their products through the supermarkets' screening mechanism and onto a good place on the shelves. Commonly called "the battle for shelf space," this process involves a great outlay for trade and public promotions, advertising pressure, and attempts to "force" distribution, along with an undertow of bribes, kickbacks, and other maneuvers. The problems involved are getting worse, and again point to the effects of new-product saturation.

When supermarkets decide to stock a new product they are increasingly inclined to throw out the weakest seller in that manufacturer's line.[*12] This coming and going is particularly noticeable in the frozen food department. How irritating it can be to the shopper is shown by this snatch of dialogue from the trade journal *Chain Store Age:*[13]

SHOPPER: I notice you're out of the frozen chicken and dumplings I bought last week. When will you have it again?
MANAGER: Oh, we've discontinued that item, Ma'am.
SHOPPER: Discontinued it? It's a brand new item!
MANAGER: Why don't you try our frozen noodle and meat ball entree? It just came in.
SHOPPER: Frankly, my family liked the dumplings. Maybe I'll try the noodles next week.
MANAGER: You'd better try it now. By next week we may have discontinued it, too!

Professor Neil H. Borden Jr., who spent two years studying the mechanism by which supermarkets accepted or rejected new products,[14] found that the expenses of failure usually must be borne by the remaining items in the line. In the case of breakfast cereals, where the introduction and failure rates are extremely high, the load is shared by gradually and repeatedly raising retail prices. Sometimes prices do not actually go up, but they are not lowered, even when successful products have built up big enough sales for this to be possible or desirable. This is one reason that heavily advertised national brands are more expensive than their private label counterparts.

Very often advertising appropriations are switched from successful products to help launch new ones, which certainly does not help, and may indeed hinder, current sales. If the flunk is monumental enough, company profits suffer. For example, Campbell Soup's failure to break Lipton's hold on the dry soup market and Heinz's share of the European market piled up losses for several years, and was one reason for the February 1967 price increase, the first in a decade.

Even if a new product "succeeds," its contribution to company profits is slight. Only 30 percent break even after their first year of full marketing, and many hardly earn anything until the end of the second year. Innovative products only pay their way by the end of the third year, though the company will probably make a killing later on. The poorest performers of all are cold breakfast cereals: only four out of ten break even after four years.

Food stores are also incurring higher costs because of the brand explosion. While the direct costs of handling new products are generally paid by the manufacturer in the form of advertising and other allowances, stores have to pay staff to consider the fifty to one hundred new products they are offered each week. They have had to increase selling areas, warehouse space, and their investment in expensive refrigeration, and improve their inventory control and handling, all of which are major factors behind their reduced turnover and higher operating costs. Many have been moaning for years about the flood of new products, particularly the marginal ones, and would doubtless agree with the comment that "today's supermarket has become a stupormarket—an environment which is not conducive to impulse buying, because of the crowded conditions of the shelves."[15] The public also has to pay this particular bill in the form of higher margins, one of the principal reasons that supermarkets are no longer fulfilling their original promise as low-cost outlets.

In view of the high cost and trouble associated with new products, it seems odd that so many manufacturers keep coming out with them. The most obvious motive is profit: The winner of this enormous crap game can indeed make a small fortune. The Green Giant Co. so successfully marketed boil-in-the-bag vegetables with butter sauce that sales in this category rose from $3 million in 1961 to $18 million three years later, and now amount to $41 million, or 23 percent of the company's total sales.

Even if they do not always hit the jackpot, companies with a consistent record of successful new products also tend to have higher than average profits. Processors like to spread the normal manufacturing risk by diversifying into fast-growing food categories, and to extend the production line. This is why cookie and cracker manufacturers keep turning out more of the same, why a canner like Del Monte, whose business tends to be seasonal, will break into the fruit drink market, and why every firm which can do so is now making snack products.

These economic reasons also generate the me-tooism. One innovative product inspires a flood of imitators who try to enlarge the total market or cut down the leader's share of it, or both. Following them are the private-labelers, particularly grocery chains, who watch carefully to see if the new product will be a winner, and if so come out with a cheaper version of their own.

Stores also have the profit motive in mind. Not only can they make booming sales out of a real winner, but new products tend to have higher margins (23 percent compared to 19.3 percent for an established grocery product) and higher retail prices. The average price of a newcomer is 34.7¢, 1.1¢ more than a survivor, and 4.5¢ more than an item which has been withdrawn. Unfortunately the stores can be bludgeoned into taking new products. Many manufacturers now try to "force" distribution by massive advertising in all media to create demand, knowing that no store will risk the possibility of hordes of screaming women and children, all preferring to fight than switch.

A good question is where Mrs. Housewife fits into this merry carousel. Despite the food industry's public protestations, the notion that her part in the birth of a new product is more than a passive one is just another myth.

There seems little respect of stopping the supermarket cornucopia from being overfilled at an ever increasing rate. During the next ten years a four hundred percent increase is expected in the flood of new products, one-third of which will actually be duplicates. One reason, which is both cause and effect of this explosion, is that new products have a shortened life-cycle. During the early sixties, the period necessary for a new product to start showing a profit was halved to about two years or less. After that, products have to be pepped up, like an aging woman, with extra advertising and promotion, new packaging, a price reduction, or reformulation in order to achieve a mere 50–50 chance of increasing sales. Like Solomon Grundy, they are born on Monday and dead by the weekend, and their death and burial can be an extremely costly process.

A more fundamental reason is the way in which our free enterprise economy operates. In times of boom there are more "go" than "stop" signs. There are no external and precious few internal controls to prevent every manufacturer from doing his thing, and no way by which excess productivity or wasteful activity can be diverted to more useful channels. Most businessmen and economists are hooked on the belief that an enterprise must grow, or die. They cannot conceive of a middle road between boom or bust, hence the recurrent fears of depression and ritual taking of the economy's temperature. Lacking any criterion of success other than crude dollars, most industrialists would view the idea of a company being satisfied with a fair or moderate profit as ludicrous or medieval.

Apart from mergers, the ability to push successful new products is a *sine qua non* of this growth process. As Kraftco (formerly the National Dairy Products Corp.) stated in its 1967 annual report, "Innovation is as important to business as high-energy foods to a growing child. It provides business with day to day vitality, it spurs the development of new and better products, new technology, better ways of doing business. It is the foundation of future profits and growth." The alternative is a horrid one: stagnation, then sliding sales, slithering on the stock market, whispering in the board room, sneers in the trade press, angry shareholders, and a one-way ticket to Siberia (or Miami) for the company president.

Hence the solution is for business to try a little harder. First and most visibly, companies must advertise. In 1968, the latest year for which figures are available, food, beer, soft drink, and candy manufacturers spent $2.4 billion on advertising and promotion. Retailers' advertising amounted to $800 million, of which about one-third was paid by the manufacturers in the form of advertising allowances. The industry total was about $2.9 billion, or $14.50 for every man, woman, and child in the country.[16]

This expenditure—one-sixth of all advertising by all U.S. corporations—enabled the industry to dominate the media to a noticeable degree. Food and related corporations were the number one spot advertisers on TV, number one on radio, number two on network TV and in newspapers, and number three in magazines. Most of this advertising was done by some 30 large companies, and cost them an average of 3.9 percent of sales.[17] It accounted for 20 percent of all advertising done by the nation's top 125 advertisers. Heading the list of these giants were: General Foods, $154,000,000; Coca-Cola, $74,000,000; Standard Brands, $65,000,000; General Mills, $58,785,000; Kraftco, $58,120,000; and the Kellogg Co., $47,000,000.

These big expenditures are caused by increasing media costs, the race to introduce new products, what competitors are doing, sheer size, and the need to maintain a big share of the market. Other factors are the need for big companies to act big, a kind of status reinforcement, of which advertising is the visible symbol, and the common practice of increasing appropriations when sales are good.

Expenditures are noticeably heaviest when the market is highly concentrated, and the giants slug it out in the hope of increasing both total consumption and their brands' lead in the race for sales. Where the market is also fairly inelastic, i.e., people do not start buying much more simply because the price drops, as in the case of cold breakfast cereals and coffee, the slugfest becomes even more frenzied. Manufacturers either launch more and more new products in the hopes of making them stick, or go all out to push existing ones, trying to survive in the crowded marketplace. The result is some appropriations which, to the layman, appear truly staggering, all the more so because most of them are divided between rival products made by the same firm. (See Appendix 5.)

Behind all this throat-cutting, attempts are also going on to make advertising less shotgun, using motivation research, copy-testing, product-testing, and mini-marketing. So far, the results are only patchily encouraging. Test marketing is said by industry to be getting better all the time, though its deficiencies are still the most likely cause of failed products. Advertising still has a strong element of whistling in the dark because of the tremendous number of variables involved. No one has yet been able to prove a really satisfactory correlation between advertising volume and sales increases,[18] much less its ability to start or stop major consumer trends such as shopping habits or tastes in food. More research would doubtless help. Most companies spend 3–6 percent of their advertising budget on research, but if they were prepared to spend 10 percent the effectiveness of advertising might be *increased* by 15–20 percent, and advertising expenditure *decreased* by 25 percent.[19]

There is also a strong possibility that advertising, in general, is becoming less effective because there is so much of it.We are now exposed to 78 messages a day, 28,470 a year, of which 84 percent are unnoticed and many of the rest regarded as irritating.[20] Here, too, our defenses are up with a vengeance—a situation that admen laconically call the "fatigue factor" but which is really our best instinct for self-preservation in a commercial world.

Advertising which gets away may still lodge in the unconscious and later produce sales. Nevertheless many advertising people are increasingly alarmed that so few messages appear to be getting through and even those that penetrate may flounder. Today's more affluent, better educated, and more sceptical consumers do not believe the propaganda to which they are daily exposed.*[21]

This crisis of confidence is far from new. We have always been sceptical of advertising, and during the last thirty years our basic attitudes have changed very little. We endorse advertising's basic economic aspects, are critical of its social aspects, and question the content and tone of the advertisements themselves—that is, when we can rouse ourselves from our boredom with the subject to express an opinion. Recent shifts of feeling have, if anything, been less favorable, especially among younger, better educated people, who very soon will be the majority of the population.[22]

All this raises the question of how much money is being spent merely to get through people's perceptual barriers and blot out competitors who are trying to do the same thing. How much advertising of overlapping products like beer, coffee, and soft drinks really enlarges *anybody's* market, and how much is merely canceled through repetition?

The fact that competition has a jamming effect is clearly seen in the test marketing field, where tactics by rival companies and the jostling of too many products distort results so that they are unreliable or unusable. Foul play is on the increase. When Procter & Gamble was testing a new Duncan Hines cake frosting in Phoenix, General Mills promptly rushed in with a new Betty Crocker frosting, same type, same coupon. "After protracted warfare, the Duncan Hines frosting was withdrawn, never to find its way into mass marketing. The Betty Crocker frosting sold well. . . ."[23] On another occasion a coffee firm hustled its cheapest grade of coffee into a new can similar to the one which a rival was test marketing, cut the price, and sold it in the same test city.

This whole wasteful and vicious competitive climate is undermining some of the economic justifications which advertising people so often cite in their own defense, and which the general public, however critical they may be about advertising's silliness, tend to take as gospel. The main arguments on advertising's behalf are, first, that it sells new products which are better than the old, and second, that by enlarging the market, it stimulates economic growth. Both points are dangerous generalizations at best. In the case of food only a few of the thousands of "new" products are new in the sense of innovative, while the extent to which they are "better" is extremely debatable.

Advertising is powerless to expand the market for food much beyond the limits of the national population increase because of the physical limits of the human stomach. Each of us gets through 1,436 lbs. of food a year, hardly more than people ate fifty years ago. Were we to gorge ourselves we would get sick or fat—a factor which puts food at a disadvantage compared with many consumer goods which we can be persuaded to buy more of and use up faster, or which can be made to break down more quickly.

Neither has advertising taught us overmuch about nutrition. While some companies and trade associations produce excellent educational material, it only crops up in ads when manufacturers feel it will be a selling point, e.g., for milk and orange juice. Since very few magazines, and still fewer newspapers or tv programs feel it is their business to teach nutrition, the result is that the average person does not know the difference between a calorie and vitamin C. This lack of knowledge is an especial handicap in view of the welter of convenience, diet, snack, and non-foods to which we are exposed, and helps account for the fact that many of us are worse nourished than we were ten years ago. (See Chap. 11.)

Advertising's principal achievement has been to sell us more services and more convenience—the little maid and now the chef lurking in almost every package. The increased tempo of modern living has created a market for convenience products. Nearly one-third of the women in the U.S. work outside their homes, and many of them find the mental effort of planning meals exceedingly boring. Advertising convinces the housewife to pay handsomely for the extra services which account for a good deal of the widening spread between farm and retail prices.

This process is not without its economic dislocations. As people eat more cold cereals and instant breakfasts they eat fewer eggs and bacon, and the farmers start screaming. As coffee creamers and non-dairy toppings take over half the cream market, dairy farmers begin to wonder whether the cow may not be doomed to obsolescence. On one hand, new processing methods can result in more convenient products and create new outlets for agriculture;

e.g., potatoes, which many people prefer not to fix from scratch, but will eat frozen, chipped, or instant mashed. On the other, the introduction of imitation and synthetic products, such as margarine, saccharin (and cyclamates, used as artificial sweeteners in soft drinks until the ban in 1969), and orange or juice drinks, has put the producers of butter, sugar, oranges, and concentrate in a spin, and led them to increase their advertising in the hopes of halting the new sales trend.*[24]

A side effect of the growth of advertising expenditures, particularly those for TV, has been a change in the pattern of competition which works in favor of the food giants. Some experts[25] believe that the high cost of advertising deters newcomers from entering grocery manufacturing and local or regional firms from "going national." On the other hand, the advantages of mass advertising have certainly spurred the merger movement in the food industry.

In 1968, the top 50 advertisers bought 89.5 percent ($943.4 million) of all network TV; out of this, 19 food and related manufacturers accounted for 25 percent.[26] A company like General Foods, with $43 million to spend, is not likely to be allowed to cool its heels in the lobby. It will be given the pick of the "packages" of programs best suited to its needs, the cream of prime viewing time, first crack at the new season's sponsorships, and a chance to renew the successes and junk the failures. Other bonuses, which smaller companies do not necessarily get, are the chance to exclude rival products from programs in the same series and the opportunity to have "piggyback" ads, minute spots divided to feature two companies in the same group, such as Pepsi and Frito-Lay. It is likely that big advertisers have comparable advantages in other media.[27]

How does the food industry's competitive situation affect the consumer? The good things, stressed often enough by the industry, are obvious: variety, some new and improved products, the security of a brand name, and information—a mixture of new-product news, receipes, and repetitious blah which is more kindly

regarded by the public than most other kinds of advertising, probably because food has so many pleasant associations.

For many people there is also the enjoyment of the "free" media
subsidized in great measure by our food dollar. The industry
helps sponsor most of the TV programs which make the top Nielsen
ratings, some news, a lot of children's programs, and a handful of
beauty contests. It makes a heavy contribution to sporting events,
particularly the National Football League and major league base-
ball. It provides between one-third and one-fifth of the advertising
revenues enjoyed by TV, radio, magazines (particularly women's),
local newspapers, and transit advertising.

If nothing else, food industry advertising and the competitive
situation which gives rise to it creates work. Food advertising alone
supports between one-sixth and one-seventh of the nation's advertising agencies[28] plus an unknown number of people employed
in food firms' advertisment departments. The product explosion
also accounts for a goodly percentage of food manufacturers' research and development, production facilities, salesmen, motivation and marketing research, and the packaging industry.

So far it has not been the American way to ask seriously how
well all these people are spending their time, or if we get good
value for the $14.50 spent by the industry to communicate with each
of us. Nor do we speculate whether ours may not be rather a poor
way to provide "free" TV; we have achieved a high level of both
technical competence and all-around silliness, poor news programs,
and a tendency for manufacturers to influence what we shall see.
Might we not get better results by paying the program companies
directly to provide a few more adult programs, perhaps on the lines
of the BBC or the Corporation for Public Broadcasting, which went
on the air in 1969?

Our payment is made in higher food prices, in the direct subsidy
of industry advertising (the whole $2.9 billion is deductible from
taxable income as one of the costs of doing business) and a portion
of our subsidy for junk mail.*[29] As a levy on our food bill, the

total cost is $58 a year, or 3 percent of the annual expenditure for a family of four. These costs fall most heavily on the poor. They are the ones who most need tax revenue diverted to social, educational, housing, and work projects on their behalf, and the least likely to work in advertising agencies or in food research and development. They also need the cheapest food, yet, ironically, are the most susceptible to the appeal of national brands, and spend millions of dollars more than necessary trying to acquire success symbols of a society which excludes them.

There are also effects not translatable in terms of money—the industry's grip on the media, the packaging jungle, the tinkering with product weight and quality which undermines brand name security, the shopping experience which is steadily sliding towards a hypnotic trance, and the irritation of coping with children brainwashed by TV advertising.

These things are important because they affect every shopper, whether or not she wonders why shopping can be such a drag or why prices keep going up. They also cast serious and specific doubts on whether our free enterprise society handles the problems of abundance as well as people think, whether the waste of resources is an inevitable part of industry operations, and if not, what can be done to improve the situation—without, of course, sending us all to Albania.

Four

THE SUPERMARKET CASINO

To many people today, "redemption" means trading in your green stamps.

A LUTHERAN MINISTER

When Mrs. Marlene Chapla, speaking for the Denver housewives said, "We're sick and tired of excuses, and we're fed up with free dishes, bingo games, and trading stamps. All we want is lower prices," the food industry had a unique chance to explain super-market economies to an eager audience. They might even have shut the ladies up for good. Instead, they muffed it, producing a lame story, the gist of which was: "It's not *my* fault."

The women would have gotten some of the missing message had they been able to tune into the 1966 convention of the Cana-dian Federation of Retail Grocers. John F. Lewis, president of Marketing Factors, Minnesota, reminded the gathering that no-body was making more profit than five years before; if anything, rather less.[1] "But we've added promotions, stamps, contests, and have built stores that are monuments to our own egos . . . all these things have been directly reflected in higher margins and higher prices of the goods we sell. . . . There are more supermarkets than there are customers to shop them."

Proliferation of stores began in the late thirties as chains hustled to take advantage of the sweet profits to be made out of super-marketing, profits which were a third or more higher than they are now.*2 They enlarged their own stores, gobbled up independents, then followed the middle-class exodus to the suburbs, settling in the new shopping centers, where two-thirds of all new super-markets are still being built. Between 1948 and 1963 the number of supermarkets*3 nearly tripled. They are still growing, but only by a thousand a year now.

Today the market is crowded enough in certain areas for *Supermarket News* to ask, and not in jest, "How about a supermarket on every block?"4 Complaints are nationwide about "overbuilding" or "overstoring," the name given to running up more outlets than the market will stand. Much of the trouble is that chains snap up a good site in a promising area, then hope that the population will catch up. Meanwhile the budding store is subsidized, either out of profits from private brands, from the operating revenue of established stores, or both.

With so many grabs being made for the same pie, individual slices have shrunk. Profits dwindled (see Appendix 2), and so did the clientele. The supermarket that could count on a population of 11,000–12,000 customers in 1954 served only 3,600 in 1968. And the number of supermarkets within reach of a typical family went up from two or three to five or six.

Investment in new stores is now almost as risky as in new products. Each year they cost more to build because of inflation, spreading parking lots, and ballooning buildings. They make smaller sales than established markets.5 And they can easily fail. Most new stores now have anywhere from one to ten competitors within a one-mile radius.

Food marketing in general has become so tight that it is difficult to grow except at someone else's expense. Thus promotions—the socially acceptable, all-American form of bribery, which always comes into play when people have too much choice—have grown to the proportions of a Thanksgiving feast. Every month, U.S. retailers have the choice of two to three hundred different ones, which manufacturers hope will persuade Madam first to sample, then to buy their darlings regularly. The bill of fare includes advertising and display allowances,[*6] point-of-purchase and display material, free offers, premiums (merchandise at a special price or free), coupons, cents-off, contests, and sweepstakes.

Stores, meanwhile, are going all out to lure Mrs. Housewife into their particular emporium, in the hope that she will do *all* her shopping there rather than with competitors. The main bait is the advertised special, or, in discount stores, well-publicized low, low prices. Trading stamps, though past their heyday,[*7] are still given by 40 percent of all supermarkets; 42 percent of the largest firms and some divisions of all top ten chains give them. Games have come out of their post-boycott doghouse, though not to their fall 1966 level, when the number of markets playing something was five times as many as now.

Other familiar tactics are premiums, particularly the continuity sort, which keep Madam coming back to complete that set of china or multi-volume cookbook. Depending on the time of year and the ingenuity of the operator, retailers also offer a variety of in-store promotions: sampling, Halloween displays, barbecues, and (with manufacturer cooperation) a stream of National Something Weeks.

As the promotion boom developed, so did the complaints from the boycotting housewives, from sophisticated consumers (called "consumerists" by the industry), from Betty Furness (then the President's Special Assistant for Consumer Affairs), and from the President's Consumer Advisory Council. Enthusiasm for stamps waned among ordinary shoppers. Since 1965 the Burgoyne Index has recorded a growing belief that stores with stamps charge higher prices, a dwindling interest in licking and sticking, and a preference by three-quarters of all shoppers for a 2 percent decrease in prices.[8] Games and contests were also viewed with a more jaundiced eye. In 1968 only 7 percent of shoppers liked them, compared to 19 percent three years before.

The government began to take a new, critical interest. The NCFM came out with a mildly worded but distinctly disapproving view of food industry advertising and promotion. At the height of the boycott, the Federal Trade Commission launched a two-year investigation into stamps and games.[9] In 1965 Congressman Lester Wolff (D-N.Y.) began the first of several attempts to pass a "truth in trading stamps" bill.*[10] In June–July 1968 John D. Dingell, chairman of the Subcommittee on Regulation and Enforcement Agencies of the House Select Committee on Small Business, held hearings on gas station games at the request of small dealers who were being forced to play against their will. One year later he began investigating sweepstakes, collecting such a roomful of data that the results had to be obtained by computer analysis. Many states also started or stepped up their inquiries into the stamps and games.[11]

The promotions boom also brought more work for the Federal Trade Commission and the Department of Justice. Into the dock came the Blue Chip Stamp Co. and Sperry & Hutchinson: One was found guilty of monopolizing trade, the other of restraining it. There were also some cases of illegal use of dealer allowances, where two medium-sized chains were accused of seeking, and one large manufacturer accused of granting allowances which were not available on an equal basis to all comers.[12]

The food industry still remains bitterly divided on promotions, particularly stamps and games. Some companies swear by one or the other or both; an equal number, including many small independents, will not touch them with a ten-foot pole. In the middle are others, like Safeway, who have made money out of them but found them a drag. Robert A. Magowan, chairman of Safeway Stores, said that his company used stamps only because women liked them, and added, "The man who could come up with a sound idea to get us out of the stamp business could earn himself one

million dollars from Safeway and others in the industry who feel
the same way."[13]

Aside from its competitive aspects, the great promotions debate
centered around five crucial questions. What do these promotions
really cost? To what extent does the consumer foot the bill for
them? Who, if anyone, profits from them? What does the consumer
get out of them? And what, if anything, can be done about the
situation?

Precise promotion costs are extremely hard to discover because
firms keep them a jealously guarded secret, while suppliers are
leery of talking openly to anyone who is not a potential customer.
Certain general figures are available (see Appendix 7), and what
is so striking is that promotion costs come to considerably more
than the stores' net profits. Food retailers are currently spending
a total of 2.41 percent of sales, the bulk of it for stamps.[14] In fact,
stamps and advertising constitute the second most expensive operating cost, running higher than taxes, utilities, insurance, or rent,
and exceeded only by labor.

The budget for all this hoopla comes out of the $2.9 billion spent
by food manufacturers and retailers for all advertising and promotions. Whether manufacturers are hotter for one or the other
depends on company policy and on the competitive situation in
the particular industry.[15] In principle, the customer foots the entire
bill, since promotion, like advertising, is as much a cost of doing
business as the ingredients or the labor of manufacturing. However, the extent to which each individual pays depends on the success of the promotion. If it increases sales satisfactorily, its cost
can be spread thinly enough not to burden the particular item
being promoted.

Not surprisingly, a fair number of promotions *do not* work.
According to the Reuben H. Donnelley Co., which claims to be
the nation's leading contest organizer and judge, 42 percent of the
1,400 contests held between 1934 and 1964 flopped, 18 percent got
a fair response, and 40 percent were successful. The most popular were the sweepstakes, followed by the limerick or jingle, with

the essay contest at the bottom of the heap.[16] Today this poor record has probably improved, since three-quarters of all contests are now sweepstakes. However, on the basis of these figures, it is likely that one-quarter are still downright bombs, and an additional 7–9 percent marginal.

Supermarket games have a break-even point after which everything is gravy—though no one in the business agrees as to where this point is. Games companies claim that it is a sales increase of 3.4–10 percent.[17] They also claim that actual sales increases can run from 8–35 percent, and average a juicy 20 percent while the game is in progress. Such results have indeed been achieved. But in many other cases, stores have done well to recover their costs.[18] A few have lost their shirts. The stores have to cope with a rush of customers intent on playing the game but who do not spend much, particularly when the game is new and hopes of winning run high.*[19]

In a few instances goofs have brought customer ill-will and embarrassment all around. In 1966 this happened with the games "Let's Go to the Races" and "Saturday Night at the Races" when the films were shown in the wrong order. "Winners came storming into the stores waving racing cards worth more than $100,000 in $1,000 prizes alone. In both cases an explanation and a rerun with the correct film molified most of those holding 'winning' cards."[20] During the summer of 1968, a similar slip occurred with "All Star Bingo." Chortled *Supermarket News*, not without a touch of malice: "Purity's face turns red as 125,999 shout 'Bingo!'" and the store had to run a special ad campaign to explain why the expected $8 million in prize money would not be forthcoming.

When a game has been unprofitable or merely broken even, stores are likely to try something else. They will push their promotion spending as high as 4 percent of sales,[21] and spread the extra expense among the 8,000 items in the supermarket. To what extent this actually happens is hard to determine. One study made for the Federal Trade Commission showed no correlation between price increases and games activity.[22] However, the FTC[23] found that one or two successful games in the same market would take trade away from competitors, often forcing them to start their own games, which did little more than halt their losses or at most make a small profit.

The FTC also found that companies which profited from games increased their margins slightly while they were in progress by spending more on all advertising and promotion. They passed on some of the costs to the public, principally by reducing the number of specials.

In the case of stamps, the effects of saturation are even more damaging. Hardly any retailers today can make the 12 percent extra in sales that Sperry & Hutchinson claims is the break-even point, let alone the 40 percent which the NCFM[24] found was necessary to cover costs. Firms that try to cut their losses are liable to be sued by the stamp companies for breach of contract. The industry as a whole is now in the awkward situation where stamps bring in little or no extra revenue but are retained for fear of losing customers. Stamp saving is a well-ingrained habit with 80–90 percent of the population.[25]

More important, there is a hard core of savers—perhaps one-quarter—who are so crazy about stamps that they will shop anywhere to get them. For this reason stamp-giving stores think very, very hard before trying something else. Meanwhile most of the cost is added to everyone's food bill.[26]

Where premiums are concerned, success stories cover everything from 7,000 olive recipe booklets offered through *Woman's Day* by Mario Foods, to the Corning Ware decanter offered by Maxwell House. The decanter is probably the most spectacular premium of all time; reputedly it sold 20 million in three years. On the other hand, unlucky or inept manufacturers may be left with a warehouse full of unwanted bric-a-brac, especially if they did no proper advance testing. Many shoppers would agree with E. B. Weiss[27] that premiums can be of poor value, often selected for fourteen-year-olds, rather than for an increasingly sophisticated and affluent public who already have all the steak knives they can use. A premium can also flunk by becoming too popular, like the offer of four hundred reproduction paintings which were snapped up in four days, leaving a trail of disgruntled customers who were unable to get any.

Sales increases from coupons can be substantial, particularly in the South, where two-thirds of all families are said to be regular redeemers. However, profits are limited by the low redemption rate—10 percent overall but only 2–3 percent in the case of newspapers, where foods are commonly advertised.[28] Another complication is "misredemption"—by shoppers who take the coupon without the product, by stores who will give cash for *anything*, by counterfeiters, by thieves at the printers, and by promoters who clip coupons from discarded newspapers and stolen new ones. Nationally, 7–16 percent of all coupons issued go astray,[29] costing the industry $20 million a year, despite sporadic campaigns to end the practice.

Exactly what does Mrs. Housewife get out of all this? It would seem that she has the choice of "cents in the hand" vs. "$1,000 in the bush." In the former category come stamps, premiums, coupons, and food store advertising, which at least acts as a guide to what food specials are being offered. The other choice, of course, includes contests and the majority of supermarket games. Occasionally people can have both; in places like Los Angeles competition caused by overstoring is so cutthroat that customers may be offered stamps, bonus stamps, games, and premiums simultaneously.

The main drawback to the jackpot type of promotion is that one person's chances of winning are worse than "a guy swimming the English Channel in a storm with an anchor round his neck."[30] The table on page 52 shows how they work out, both for the shopper who patronizes the store steadily throughout the game period, and for the one who drops in once on the off chance.[31]

The Federal Trade Commission found that these low theoretical chances of winning were distorted by the common practice of "rigging." Chains would arrange for several large prizes to be awarded early in the game to whip up interest, particularly if their

● Food industry overbuilding results in promotions bonanzas in which housewives may be offered stamps, bonus stamps, games, and premiums simultaneously. But in the supermarket casino, real prizes are thin on the ground. Shoppers mostly get the chore of licking and sticking, and the frustration of *not* winning at Bonus Bingo.

CHANCE OF WINNING

Prize	Regular shopper	Casual shopper
$1	1 in 10	1 in 257
5	1 in 76	1 in 1.9 million
10	1 in 240	1 in 6 million
20	1 in 148	1 in 3.7 million
100	1 in 840	1 in 21 million
500	1 in 1,704	1 in 42.6 million
1,000	1 in 11,512	1 in 287 million

game was encountering stiff competition from rivals. Also, they often saw to it that most of the $1,000 jackpots went to selected stores, again where competition was keenest. One Los Angeles store[32] was even advised by a game promoter to take the first $1,000 prize and plant it among the most talkative women in the neighborhood.

Congressman Dingell's committee found that few top prizes are handed out in the "pre-selected" type of sweepstakes, so-called because the winners are determined in advance by the sponsor rather than by a drawing. The trouble was not rigging, but merely failure to replace winning entries which, as often happens, were lost or not redeemed. Many of the lesser prizes were pure junk, and no consolation to those who bought the product in the pathetic hope of increasing their chances of winning. Armour & Co., one of seven famous food companies guilty of this petty deception, dished out 84 stuffed elephants costing a little over $2 each during its White Elephant sweepstakes. No one came within a mile of the live elephant (or $25,000), the dream vacation, or several Edsel cars.

Probably stamps offer the best value in the cents-in-hand type of promotion, since their "retail value" is about 20 percent more than the merchant paid for them. However, as everybody knows, there are minor irritations all along the line. Saving involves the bother of licking and sticking. Contrary to what many people think, the stamps remain the property of the stamp company, and can be exchanged for cash in only nineteen states*[33] (a point that stamp companies like to play down, and may even omit from the fine-print instructions in their stamp books). Patronizing a redemption center means short hours and often long lines, poor service, no delivery, and, on popular items, a chronic tendency to be out of stock. If the stamp company folds, which has happened among small firms, especially in the fifties and early sixties, consumers may be stuck with books which are partially or completely useless.

Coupons are very often more trouble than they are worth. Dr. Mabel Newcomer, a writer on consumer affairs for the Berkeley *Co-op News*, described how she had to empty a 6 oz. jar of Nescafé to get at the 55¢ in coupons at the bottom, refill the jar, with "a funnel, a spoon and patience," mail the 50¢ refund coupon at a cost of 7¢ for the stamp and envelope, and take the 5¢ coupon to her local Safeway for a reduction on a package of Total cereal, which was out of stock. The result was 17¢ for a good half hour of busywork, since the Nescafé cost 26¢ more than her usual brand of coffee. How many housewives have this sort of time?

Until early 1970, when the FTC began a crackdown, many coupon offers were also unfair and misleading. Some had an unreasonably short expiration date; others were hedged around with fine-print restrictions that consumers often missed. Either way, shoppers were conned into buying the product by the coupon, which then turned out to be worthless.

National brand premiums, whose price and quality can be ascertained, are usually a good buy. But others may be poorly made, inadequately packed, slow to arrive, and save the housewife far less than the 50 percent average that the offering company claims, thanks to a grossly inflated retail price.

For the serious shopper, all promotions are about as much fun as a stone in the shoe, mainly because they hinder price comparison and supply entertainment which is not to all tastes. Yet it requires an unusual determination *not* to go along. In fact, gambling, which is so hedged around with legal restrictions for anyone who wants to do it seriously, is practically a mandatory part of food shopping. All the customers get game cards shoved at them as they go through the checkout, whether they want them or not, and many people save stamps only because they are worth too much to leave on the counter. To say to non-players and non-savers "shop somewhere else" may not be entirely realistic. If most or all of the competing supermarkets in the area are offering some kind of promotion, there is nowhere to shop, except at a "mom and pop," or miles out of the way.

More worrisome is the fact that all promotions provide the opportunity for enterprising businessmen to add a new layer of what are euphemistically called "services" to the food marketing bill, and make a handsome profit in the process. Some professional promotions firms have begun taking over the games companies, which began as small, get-rich-quick operations.[34] A number of food chains have worked their way into the stamp business, setting up "captive" companies like Blue Chip (started by nine California chains), Top Value Enterprises (Kroger Co.), Merchants Green Stamp Co. (Food Fair), and Stop & Save Trading Stamp Co. (Grand Union). After these "captives" get into the swing of the business, they may even become full-fledged promotion companies, like Blue Chip, which went public and began testing its own supermarket game.

The spillover effects of the supermarket casino business are considerable. The $3 billion a year premium industry disposes of some 30 percent of all the china manufactured in this country, 20 percent of the aluminum-ware, and 15 percent of the glassware. It also supports special departments of many leading manufacturers, a scattering of small fry who grind out premium merchandise, and the premium houses that dispose of it. Big stamp companies buy as much or more as large department stores; they also contract for a good deal of paper and printing services.

How much money do stamp and games companies make? It is likely that out of the 200 stamp and 39 games firms*[35] many fringe companies operate on a shoestring, or even in the red.[36] On the other hand, profits at the upper end of the scale are probably substantial. Until 1967 Sperry & Hutchinson's return on investment—35 percent after taxes[37]—was double that of a conventional department store and three and a half times that of a food chain. These figures might lead the average consumer to wonder why green stamp savers could not get a better "price break" on merchandise. Blue Chip Stamp Co., until 1969 a private, nonprofit corporation, has tucked away a good many millions, and a $10 share purchased in 1956 is now worth about $50,000.[38]

The key factor in stamp company profits is their sizeable "float" —the interest-free money in their possession from the time the retailers purchase the stamps until the customers redeem them. A second is the fact that not all stamps are redeemed. The stamp companies pay income tax on a theoretical redemption rate of 95 percent, but the actual rate is probably 80–90 percent, which constitutes a significantly lower business expense.[39] The stamp companies claim that their prices and the redemption value of the merchandise are set with this gap in mind; Congressman Wolff for one claims that they are getting a bonus of $50 million a year, interest free.

Less is known about games company operations. However, the FTC found that their total revenue jumped from $2.7 million in 1963 and $8.4 million in 1965, to $37.2 million in 1966. Seventy percent of the market is held by four leading companies;[40] one of them, Glendinning, founded in 1960, has enjoyed sales increases ranging from 37 percent to 221 percent a year since 1962.

Profits can pile up in two ways: first, from the cost of the game itself. At least one games operator[41] believes that the $10 per 1,000 cards that some companies charge is much too high, even for games with a good "track" record, since the actual cost may be no more than $5. Second, the stores have to purchase about 30 percent extra in cards to cover additional traffic. This can come to 24,000–30,000 cards per store during a normal game period, at a maximum cost of $240–$300.

From both the public and the industry point of view, more research is needed on precisely those competitive conditions under which different types of promotions *do not* work, and must therefore be added to the food bill.

However, all the information in the world will not alter the fact that there are too many stores—and none of them want to lie down and die. The industry is trapped in an endless promotional cycle, from which neither common sense nor self-regulation can free it. A promotion is tried and proves successful while only a limited number use it. As more firms climb on the bandwagon, it begins to lose its efficacy, and not until enough people drop it will it start working once more. This cycle has been clearly seen in stamps and games. At the time of writing, they had reached a fairly low ebb, but many retailers believed they might soon start rolling again. The industry's mood is one of disenchantment. Super Market Institute executive director Michael O'Connor said, "I think the promotional devices that we've been using in this business in the last several years are running out of gas. . . . We don't have a major new device to build volume with."[42]

A commonsense question at this point, which housewives are never tired of asking, is why not give promotions a rest and simply lower prices by 2 percent? Indeed, some food chains are to a limited extent following this solution. Since the 1966 boycotts, when the consumer message about low prices began to get through, the move to discount operations has been quite striking. All over the country chains have started to experiment in some of their divisions, either changing over to complete discount (reduced hours, variety, staff, and price cuts across the board) or more commonly, lowering prices on the few hundred staple items which Madam can remember.

It has been conceded that "cutting out stamps and games could reduce prices 2.5 percent without affecting profit."[43] Why doesn't everybody do it? In the first place, even if food retailers could agree to do so, any collective action to drop promotions would violate the antitrust laws.[44] Barred from what is perhaps the obvious solution, companies would have to make the decision on their own, and

competition being what it is, no one is prepared to risk being clobbered by his rivals. Even dropping stamps in favor of reduced
prices is a bigger risk than many companies feel they can take.
A number who have done so have suffered depressed profits for
several months, or even lost so much money that they had to bring
stamps back a year later.

If dropping promotions would be a gamble, universal price
cutting would be suicide. Many of today's affluent consumers are
not particularly sensitive to price cuts under 5 percent. Where
certain foods are concerned they are not sensitive at all, and these
products would practically have to be given away before people
would eat much more. Food stores, operating on just under a 1
percent profit, can only manage deep cuts on a limited number of
items, while 5 percent across the board would put them all out of
business. Hence, price cutting will be successful on a restricted
scale only. As a promotion, both retailers and manufacturers will
use it to the extent that they can gain extra sales volume and
profits, and even then, with the greatest reluctance, as it is all
too easy for competitors to retaliate and start destructive price
wars.

As long as promotions work, the food industry will go on using
them—and they work up to a point because they are firmly rooted
in the psychology of a substantial number of people. They may
never number more than 20–30 percent of the population at any
one time, but they are important enough to result in *everyone* being
offered stamps, games, coupons, or three steak knives for $1. The
lure of stamps is both delicate and complex. They are a built-in
bank for people who cannot save, and a nest egg for wives without much mad money. They appeal simultaneously to the instinct
for thrift and the need to splurge, promising both something for
nothing and a chance to get that delicious, luxurious extra that
conscience or a tight budget would not otherwise permit.

Games and contests appeal, not, as might be supposed, to the
hidden gambler in people, but to the child, who rebels occasionally
at having to be responsible and self-sufficient. According to How-

ard Brown, vice president of a successful games firm (the Plaza Group), who has written a book on games psychology: "When we were children we always got something for nothing. But when we're older, it's different—you get nothing for nothing. In games, here's an opportunity to re-experience that early developmental level of getting something free. You match something, and you get a reward."

How can we escape from ever increasing amounts of advertising, and from an endless cycle of promotions which boom, drone, and then bust?

The industry solution is to try a little harder, to make advertising work by increasing the quantity, and by trying, through improvement or packaging, to differentiate the product. At the retail level, no stone is left unturned for a promotion that is a traffic stealer, at least temporarily.

Unfortunately, industry can do little or nothing to change the competitive situation which has gotten it onto this treadmill. From time to time industry spokesmen exhort each other to cut down on some of the me-toos, to use better marketing research and electronic data processing to give survivors a better chance, and not to stifle the local retail markets by opening too many new stores. While this is all sensible advice which individual companies might want to follow, it would only work if everybody did it, e.g., by setting up a cartel. This is, of course, illegal, and would probably result in all kinds of undesirable price-fixing and restraint of trade.

Rather more could be done on the outside by government action:

The NCFM *suggested that "Consumer grades should be developed and required to appear on all foods for which such grades are feasible," in order "to inform consumers . . . and reduce the excessive use of promotion, thus contributing to a better performance of the food industry."*[45]
Truth in trading stamps.
Truth in promotions.

An outright ban on stamps and games of chance.

Limit tax deductions on excessive expenditures by food firms for advertising, merchandising, and packaging (a drastic measure proposed by Congressman Paul Fino [R–N.Y.] in 1966).[46]

These ideas were approved in principle by the White House Conference on Food, Nutrition and Health.

The only measure implemented so far is a partial truth in promotions. New FTC rules, effective October 1969, prohibit games rigging and deceptive advertising which misleads consumers about their chances of winning. The public must now be told the exact number of prizes available and their distribution in specific geographic areas.

There is an obvious case for truth in trading stamps and full truth in promotions. Such information would provide valuable guidance for people who want to shop rationally, who want the facts about these types of promotions, or the cash alternative. It would not destroy the appeal of stamps for ardent savers or games for ardent players. There is a case for limiting tax deductions for marketing and other expenditures, possibly varying within different product categories. Some other arrangements could also be made to finance the media, particularly TV, whose revenues would certainly suffer.

What can ordinary shoppers do while waiting for Godot? In the first place, they could give a lot more political support for legislators' proposals to regulate the food industry so that the federal government can *really* fulfill its watchdog functions. They could exert a great deal more leverage on food industry operations—a leverage that the food boycotts showed was possible, though without the fatigue and frustration of forming picket lines and waving banners. As noted earlier, each type of industry promotion plays to a relatively small gallery—perhaps one-third of the customers are enthusiastic at any one time. Hence it would take no more than one-third of the shoppers *expressing their dislike openly and threatening to take their custom elsewhere* to put stores and manufacturers in such a dilemma that they would reconsider and perhaps change their promotion policies. If one-third of the women refuse their stamps, refuse their game cards, and tell the store manager that they will shop elsewhere if these promotions are not discontinued, they will get their way at least in their marketing area—for what store manager can risk losing one-third of his good customers? A similar tactic might also be successful if enough women wrote to the manufacturers of their favorite brands, informing them that they will certainly switch until the premiums, contests, and coupons are dropped.

The effect on the food bill will not be magical. Even dropping all retail promotions would only lop 2½ percent from the food bill, or about $47 a year for an average family of four. However, it would also end the irritation of licking, sticking, and not winning at games, and possibly induce a few more stores to go into discount operations, which could save another 3 percent.

People who like food industry promotions, but prefer the cents-in-the-hand variety, can maximize their value by shopping around for premium and stamp merchandise as carefully as they would for any other. Where premiums are concerned, it is wise to stick to reliable national brands, provided the savings are better than the local discount store can provide (unless the offer looks like a steal at any price). Before redeeming stamps—unless the urge to splurge outweighs any price considerations—it helps to consult *Consumer Reports* to check on the reliability of the item. It also helps to compare prices since all stamp merchandise is not equal in value.

A fairly safe rule of thumb is that stamp books are worth rather less than the issuing companies claim. S. & H. says that its books have a retail value of around $3, 21 percent more than the merchant paid for the stamps, with an actual range of $2 to more than $5. The latest and biggest survey on the subject,[47] covering 200 items in six cities during late 1966, showed a range of $1.50 to $6.72, and an average value of $3.25; the equivalent in a department store would be $3.05, or $2.79 at discount. The survey also showed that many of the most popular items were "priced" at less than par. Taking $3.25 per book of green stamps as the norm, here is how they worked out:

Items below par	*Value per book*
small appliances and radios	$2.62
sheets and towels	2.76
bath items	2.92
luggage	3.02
linens	3.06
sporting goods	3.11
tools	3.19

Items at par	
toys and juvenile items	3.24
china	3.31

Items above par	
furniture, lamps, picnic and garden supplies, jewelry, clothing, silver, hollow ware (serving dishes), and flatware (cutlery)	3.45 and up

For people who want to win at games, the author has no advice —except that if you can manage to work out a system for spotting the $1,000 winners, find a good attorney and be sure the games company settles out of court for a generous price.*[48]

F
ive

THE SHOPPING MAZE

The woman shopping in the supermarket is often a woman totally confused.

GENERAL MANAGER
Ralph's Grocery Co., Los Angeles

Complicating the crowded conditions under which it operates, the food industry is now facing a unique and troublesome marketing challenge. According to Clarence G. Adamy, president of the National Association of Food Chains: "We have an obligation to keep prices for food as low as possible, because it is, after all, essential to life. But at the same time, we have every right to encourage people—as other retailers—to trade up to things that are beyond the basics. Why shouldn't steaks compete with a new car or a bigger house, or a boat?"[1]

Despite steady price increases, food expenditures have neither kept pace with the cost of living nor our increasing affluence. We spend a small proportion, 16.8 percent[2] of net income, at the grocery store, a trend common to advanced countries.

Not only do we not eat more, but we are distinctly capricious as to where we spend our money, a quality the industry calls "disloyalty." The majority of shoppers (sensibly) divide their custom between two, three, or even more stores. Every year there is a partial reshuffle as 20 percent of the families move from their neighborhoods. Food retailers are kept perpetually wondering (irrationally?) how much patronage they can continue to expect.

A major reason for this "disloyalty" is that, with a growing number of exceptions, one large supermarket is pretty much like the next. One day back in 1959, a food chain president visited a local manager and conducted the whole interview without realizing that this was not his manager and the store was not even part of his company.[3] In private the industry also concedes that stores are not only very much alike, but that they can be unattractive and confusing. One trade magazine said the customer "sees a store that is drab by comparison with her own home. She sees a store whose lighting produces so much glare that it hurts her eyes. She feels cold walking down the frozen food aisle . . . do the cold, the glare and the drabness put her in a buying mood—*in a big buying mood?* Not hardly!"[4]

Can women be persuaded to spend more by selling them not merely food but meals, status, a touch of luxury, and a pleasant shopping experience? Marketing experts, opinion researchers, food manufacturers, store managers, university professors, and newspaper and magazine editors have been having a fine field day looking for the answers.

The first stage has been to study women and how they tick, particularly how they shop, and what they look for in a food store. What has emerged at the initial level is a statistical profile of the "average" shopper: She spends 27–29 minutes on a typical shopping trip, buys $7.31 worth of merchandise (adding up to a total of $30–$45 for the week's shopping, plus $2–$3 for overlooked items), likes to shop weekends, patronizes two or three different stores, grumbles about waiting at the checkout, would like more service but cannot get it, rates a store most highly for quality meats and produce but will quit it if prices are too high.

What has also been learned is that there is no "average shopper." For example, the high-income consumer (earning $15,000 a year or more) wants the best quality and the best service, and can pay for it. She spends more per capita for food than any other group (an average of $45 a week for her family) and is less interested in low prices, though on occasions can be a tough, shrewd bargain hunter. She likes new, particularly convenience foods. Her pets have the biggest appetites. She expects a clean, attractive store, and if the bag-boy is rude to her she may never come back.

Mrs. Newlywed is also a heavy spender, probably because she works. She is not particularly bargain-conscious, lacking the time or energy to hunt for specials. She likes to shop on Saturdays, half the time accompanied by her husband, with whom she will spend a couple of dollars more than if she were on her own. Though she says she likes to cook, she is extremely uncertain how to select fresh meat and produce; she also tends to buy the same brand of groceries her mother bought.

Mrs. Middle Income tends to have the biggest family, and will spend $30 or more at a crack on her weekend shopping. For her, a visit to the supermarket is most likely to be a chore, and since she puts in an 80-hour week at home, she would like to get her shopping done quickly without being given the runaround. Unlike the other two she is quite price-conscious and reads the ads and shops for specials, although she is likely to grab a stack of TV dinners instead of stew meat when time is especially short.[5]

Still more illuminating are the industry's findings about the way women shop—which are now being applied in food stores all around the country to generate extra sales. First, some 60 percent no longer make shopping lists, but wait until they are in the supermarket to decide what to buy. This leaves them open to the supermarket's suggestions. Signs, displays, and other merchandising tactics urge them to buy high-margin items for which they had not previously realized a need, and they may come out with more than they had intended.

Very few women can remember prices, mostly because of the

wild proliferation of products in today's typical supermarket. One study[6] of people's price knowledge of 60 staple items showed that the only one that the majority (86 percent) could remember accurately was a 6-pack of Coca-Cola. Thirty to 39 percent knew the prices of a handful of products ranging from Camel cigarettes to Campbell's tomato soup. The best that most people could manage was a good general knowledge (within 5 percent) of prices on some commonly bought items.

There is a diminishing need to be price-conscious, except for families on a tight budget, or during periods of rapid and noticeable price rise (like 1966 and 1969). Surveys suggest that the modern shopper is interested as much or more in high quality and convenience, and attractive, tastefully decorated stores, with courteous personnel and the maximum of service.

Though keenly interested in quality, and more able to afford it, many shoppers are extremely uncertain about how to choose it. Their knowledge of food has not caught up with fast-moving food technology and new methods of meat cutting. Many are just inexperienced, particularly today's younger brides. Publicly, the food industry remains committed to the view that the American woman is an expert shopper, "a prowling computer . . . jungle-trained, her bargain-hunter's senses razor-sharp for the sound of a dropping price."[7] Privately, industry agrees with Clarence Adamy: "More women than are willing to admit it are really frightened by the experience of shopping in a supermarket . . . the American consumer really is a troubled stranger in paradise."[8] Specifically, the industry believes that many women will not cook or do not know how to, know little about fresh produce, and find meat buying, except for roasts, steaks, or chops, a complete mystery.

All these findings have been put to work so that women get what they want and the industry will profit from it. There has been a tremendous upgrading of the physical appearance of most food stores, and a new emphasis on atmosphere. During the last decade supermarkets became 25 to 100 percent larger, provided twice or three times as much parking space as total store area, and

● Most shoppers are stymied in the supermarket money game by not being told the rules. Industry's ploy is to expose us to the maximum number of items, slow us down, and catch our eye with enticing packages, special displays, and point-of-purchase signs. Our countermove should be blinders, a shopping list, full knowledge of the tricks of the trade, and a steely determination to make shopping a rational affair instead of a trip to Las Vegas.

put in wider aisles, air conditioning, and automatic doors. Re-modeling currently proceeds at the fast clip of 3,000 supermarkets a year for chain stores alone,[9] largely because "it's cheaper and less risky to remodel an older unit that's making money than to build one in a new location that could fail."[10] Within limits of economy, architects are being given their head. Exteriors are generally grace-ful; interiors are becoming more like *Better Homes and Gardens*, with striking color schemes, modern-art cutouts over produce departments, original fixtures and fittings, improved lighting, and even wall-to-wall carpeting.

The object of all this face-lifting is to give stores a more distinct personality. In fact, "with increasingly tight competition, store design is just about the only area in which a super can be different."[11] If the decor is striking enough it will attract people from outside the mile or so radius within which they normally shop. Pleasant surroundings help Madam to relax, and concentrate better on the merchandise. They also induce her to spin out her shopping trip—and every minute she takes beyond half an hour will add 50¢ to her bill.[12]

More services are being offered for the same reasons—though here housewives are not so well provided for. What the industry has been able to persuade them to accept as "service" amounts to little more than an improvement in amenity. Shopping is a little easier but still basically a do-it-yourself operation. Most women continue to select and lug their own groceries, but they can now do it to music. They can cash checks while breathing conditioned air, often spiced with heady aromas from the in-store bakery. They can return bottles to the courtesy counter instead of waiting at the checkout, sometimes find a kiddie korner for the small fry, and then exit through automatic doors. Many of these services are now an automatic part of supermarket operation and add more to operating expense than they generate in traffic. A few of the newer ones just about pay off, e.g., the in-store bakery and delicatessen and the customer lounge and (sometimes) free coffee bar, which are designed to relax people into making longer and more profitable shopping trips.

Once inside the store, armed with a cart but no shopping list, today's housewife is now exposed to a floor layout which is a scientifically designed compromise between her need to find things easily and the store's need to induce her to spend more money than she intended. Studies of supermarket traffic patterns show that 75 percent of shoppers normally walk around the store perimeter. Here they find produce, meat, baked goods, dairy products, and often frozen foods. Partly these departments are locate here for service convenience. More important, some of them also carry a generally higher margin (see Appendix 6) than the groceries in the center maze of gondolas. By design, the store leads people to these more profitable items, especially early in the trip while they still have money. "Make as much profit as possible before the shopper discovers she has spent all her money and has to stop buying." As one store operator put it, "Anything first in line sells better. I don't know whether the shopper gets tired toward the end or has run out of money; it just seems to work that way."[13]

A second fundamental is to *expose every customer to as many items* as possible per trip."[14] The process is extremely delicate: If women are made to work *too* hard they get tired and confused, and may leave in disgust. But if they could lay their hands on what they wanted without effort, half the departments would remain unvisited, and the store would lose profitable traffic.

A well-designed layout can lure women from the beaten track of their shopping with a graceful inevitability which can make the whole safari time-consuming but pleasant. Women can be propelled the whole length of the meat counter by the judicious display of steaks, bacon, and franks. They will hunt the whole produce department in search of lettuce, potatoes, and oranges, which are cleverly divided between the main counter and displays on side tables. Around the perimeter, their attention can be transferred to the neglected opposite aisle by lighted shelving, displays, signs, new items, or merely coffee and sugar, which they wanted all along. In the mid-store wilderness the chase gets more exciting, for though they will actually *find* their familiar groceries here, they will also be exposed to a lot of other things.

What is it that the store is so insistent that women see and buy? Obviously it would like women to buy everything—but especially those items with a high margin. Some of these, like produce and certain meats, will sell themselves, but there are many impulse items which women do not normally plan to buy in advance but will do so if they see them. At the top of this list are candy, crackers, cookies, snacks, baked goods (particularly cake), frozen foods, cigarettes, magazines, and health and beauty aids; 70 to 90 percent of the time these are bought as the result of an in-store decision. Most of these items are unusually profitable for the store. Others include housewares, toys, and other general merchandise, and gourmet or fancy foods, for which turnover is low but margin is high, and are therefore profitable.

Merely exposing shoppers to those products, however, is not enough. In the mass of 8,000 items screaming for attention almost anything can get lost unless it is given star billing. "Mrs. Housewife passes 3,800 items in 12 minutes. This means she passes 317 items per minute. Must see a given product and decide to buy within 1/5th of a second. This is probably why she always buys at least one item from a special display."[15]

Occasionally such displays are store-wide, notably at seasonal festivals like Christmas, Easter, Halloween, and Thanksgiving, when the store blossoms with streamers, Santas, witches, and pumpkins, anything to help the holiday atmosphere and increase sales. The results are often rewarding but sometimes difficult to prove. In a survey of 107 executives representing 23,249 stores, *Progressive Grocer* found that nearly two-thirds of them estimated an average gain of 14.9 percent as a result of such displays.[16] Most of the others simply did not know, either because their accounting methods were not sensitive enough to catch the ebb and flow of sales, or because the results depended on too many variables, e.g., what their competitors were or were not doing at the time.

More commonly, displays push one special product group, as during National Dairy Week, when the manufacturers pile in with banners, point-of-purchase material, advertising allowances, and plaster cows; and Idaho Potato or Washington Apple week, when displays are built to stun with sheer volume. Also on the increase are ethnic or international promotions to sell gourmet foods, where the sales personnel dress up in saris, smocks, or lederhosen. The interesting point about such efforts is that they not only sell the target product, they sell related items which are tied in with the main display. One midwest dairy promotion increased dairy sales by 68 percent and cheese sales by 500 percent, but also helped sell more ham, spaghetti, crackers, cucumbers, salads, strawberries, and apples.[17]

Quite apart from all these special events, less ambitious displays are used every day of the week to sell any number of things the store wishes to push. Many of these are "end displays," i.e., on the ends of the shelves or gondolas. Because these locations naturally catch the eye, they are considered particularly choice spots for specials, high margin, and/or impulse items. Others are "tumble" or "jumble" displays, whose appeal is their sheer disorder; they never make the housewife feel guilty about disarranging a symmetrical pile of goodies to remove one.

Other devices are "product spotters"—signs, often hand-lettered, which simply draw attention to the item by giving its name, a come-on like *new! special! featured!* or *advertised*, or selected mouth-watering adjectives for meat and produce like *juicy, garden-fresh, choice,* or *good for broiling.* The implication that the shopper is getting a bargain is particularly strong, and often completely erroneous. However, the *Progressive Grocer* Colonial Study found that "special displays at regular prices sold nearly as well as similar displays offering reduced prices."

Another booby-trap is the "tie-in," based on the quite reasonable theory that the housewife thinks in terms of meals rather than individual products. This accounts for the practice of nestling salad dressings with the lettuce, bibs and talcum powder with the baby food, syrup with the pancake mix, and meat sauce with the spaghetti. Using tie-ins a store can make money at Thanksgiving: The turkeys generally sell at cost, but the nearby dressing, cranberry sauce, and decorative Indian corn make a handsome profit. Tie-ins sell a lot of housewares, which are often displayed with food products on hooks or racks, appropriately called "sore thumbs." Tie-ins also help finance store specials.

Another fundamental principle of supermarket display is that profitable items must almost fall into the shopping cart. Impulse items like cigarettes, candy, and magazines are nearly always found at the checkout, where there is an almost overwhelming temptation to flip through the latest *Reader's Digest*, or pacify the children with a 5¢ candy bar. The prize shelf location is at eye level, because it seems "there is a definite resistance every time the supermarket requires physical exertion by the customer."[18] Tests have shown that the same four items sold 63 percent more during a two-week period when they were raised from waist to eye level, and 78 percent more when they were raised from floor to eye level. Conversely, as they were moved down progressively from eye to floor level, sales dropped substantially. With children's products the optimum level is lower. If the little one can actually reach for the toy, candy, cookies, or favorite snap, crackle, and pop, *and get it into the shopping cart*, he stands a better chance of persuading mother to buy, especially if she does not discover it until she reaches the checkout.

With exotic or unfamiliar products the store will exercise more ingenuity, particularly if it has a large newlywed clientele, or is aiming for what used to be called the carriage trade. Free or nominally priced recipes provide a service for the customer and help the store sell problem merchandise—products that have a low turnover but a high margin, like fresh produce (which many young wives do not know how to cook) and novelties such as kumquats or papayas (which people of all ages may not know how to deal with). Recipes get rid of cuts of meat that make up the bulk of the carcass, but which are passed up in favor of steaks or chops, because they require longer or expert cooking.[19] Weekly meal-planning guides can increase volume in all food departments—housewives who decide to make flaming shish-kebab this week will purchase all the ingredients on the spot.

Supermarkets also experiment from time to time with more direct methods of creating need through food education. Some run successful (and much needed) classes showing how meat is cut and cooked, and classes in food marketing for high school students. Others run promotions to give customers what may be their first taste of a new frozen or specialty food. Crisply uniformed or ethnically robed hostesses will cook the product and hand around bite-sized samples to any shopper who comes within reach. "Some customers," said a Los Angeles buyer, "might 'wince at a blinz' if they'd never tried one, but now some of our best Japanese customers are blinz customers, after sampling—and they're potato pancake eaters, too."[20] More rarely, a store will really go to town. Richards Lido Market, Newport Beach, California, held a luau for 1,000 customers, laying on everything from native dancers to roast suckling pig washed down with guava juice.[21]

Completing these ways of loosening the pursestrings is a complex method of pricing, which can be summed up as the art of giving bargains while not losing money. The way it works is roughly this: All stores have to recover more or less fixed expenses, with an allowance for net profit. Certain overall price and profit targets are set for each department, on the assumption that different departments have different operating expenses and make different contributions to sales. Each department has certain items which normally sell at an extremely low margin, or none at all, partly because they are high-volume, and can pay their contribution to store expenses much more often, but also because most shoppers know their approximate price. No store dares step out of line and risk being uncompetitive by marking up coffee, sugar, or milk. What is lost on staples naturally has to be made up on the thousands of other items which have a lower turnover but a higher margin, and where the housewife is none too certain of the "regular" price. "This orchestration of prices," said the NCFM report, "creates what is referred to as the 'sales mix' . . . the best sales mix for a store would be a minimum of strategic items at low prices to bring in the traffic, and a maximum of higher priced items to increase profit."[22]

It is from the staples section, including meat, that stores normally offer specials. These are promotional price reductions and do not provoke retaliation by competitors, who are too busy offering specials of their own, but on a slightly different rotation. In its survey of nine chains in four cities, the NCFM found an average of 50 items, from a total range of 200–300, which were normally on special. Only "about one special in seven was not a reduction in price from the 'regular' price."[23] All the chains studied were more or less competitive in the way they offered specials. However, it is likely that the degree of specialing does fluctuate in different parts of the country.[24]

About three-quarters of the time some of the losses are shared by manufacturers in the form of cents-off, advertising, or other allowance. However the stores may still help redress the balance by selective price increases among their high-margin items. Alternatively they use tie-in and other displays to make sure that housewives pick up such items along with the specials.

One example taken from a classic grocery marketing textbook illustrates the planning that must go on. The item to be specialed was Tide. The expected sales were 1,600 cases (usual sales 310), at only a 16.6 percent margin, producing a loss of $1,040 instead of a profit of $208. To make up the balance required sales of $25,000 at a margin of approximately 26 percent ($6,000). This worked out to be 2,500 cases of vanilla wafers (at a margin of $3,000 or 20 percent), 1,000 cases of candy (at a margin of $2,160 or 31 percent), and 1,000 cases of pickles (at $1,080 or 32 percent).[25]

There are two other pricing techniques that supermarkets think consumers prefer, or that give the illusion of a bargain. One is "psychological pricing," in which nearly everything seems to end in a 9, because it looks cheaper. The second is multiple pricing, particularly 2 for 29¢, 6 for 79¢, or even 4 for $1. Multiple pricing induces people to stockpile, and sells substantially more than single pricing.[*26] Presumably people do not or cannot figure out that the most they usually save is 1¢, or they feel that the store will not honor the special if they split the multiple.

Shopper confusion reaches a new peak in the meat department. The butchers are "trading-up" with a vengeance by cutting and trimming familiar cuts in a multitude of different ways, giving them fancy names and selling them for 4¢ to $1.40 more per pound (median 50¢). Meat cutting varies in different parts of the country and even from store to store (see Appendix 11), but most of the new cuts are either chuck, sirloin, or round. The price increase represents partly slight differences in the primal cut (when the best bit of the chuck—the eye or fillet—is dressed up as "Jewish fillet") and partly the trim (which is usually a bit closer, or boneless, and requires a highly paid butcher). Mostly it represents pure profit for the meat department, and gives the consumer some convenience at a terrifically high cost. It also produces the familiar scene of women drifting miserably up and down the meat counter (particularly at weekends when the department is busy) trying to find someone to tell them what London Broil is and how to cook it.

Women might also very well ask "what is 'Blogg's Blue Ribbon beef'?"—another example of meat department trading-up. The fact is that "Blogg's Blue Ribbon-Gold Ribbon-Gourmet-Good-Better-Best" has no objective meaning at all. It bears no relation to any U.S. Department of Agriculture meat grade, though in high quality stores "Blogg's Finest" is mostly choice, and occasionally prime. Elsewhere it could be choice, or even a lower grade like good or standard. (See Appendix 11). It is a way out for those meat departments that "have been experimenting with two different grades . . . and even *three* grades of meat . . . and are facing the problem of how to identify one without making it appear that one is an *inferior* grade."[27]

A third type of trade-up is the "quickie meals" section, guaranteed to add an extra $200 to $1,000 a week to meat department volume. This consists of prepared items, such as "meat loaf, Salisbury steak, cabbage rolls, stuffed pepper, meat balls, taco-fill—all of which combine meat with a dehydrated meat-loaf mix and water."[28] On closer inspection, most of them are merely hamburger meat at fancy prices. The stuffed poultry or pork chops which may also be included incorporate a dry dressing mix costing Madam between 79¢ and 98¢ a lb.

In a more general attempt to upgrade, many stores are offering prime or specially tenderized meats; greater variety; cutting, marinating, and barbecuing to order; and even a real old-fashioned butcher in striped apron and straw hat. They are also raising prices to match. Others merely change the method of cutting, improve the decor, and add small gratutious touches which give the air of luxury, such as a pat of butter in every meat package, a slice of green pepper with the meat loaf, or a piece of pineapple or a cherry with every ham.

It would be easy, but unfair, to point to meat departments as the only villains. Trading-up is their answer to a continuous cost-profit squeeze, caused by higher farm and meat-packer prices, and a high store labor cost. The head butcher is second in pay only to the store manager, at least in California. A typical butcher gets 4¢–6¢ a minute, depending on where he works. Consumers, too, are partly responsible, because of their insistence on convenience of preparation and their reluctance to use the carving knife.

Today's meat department is merely the bellwether for a new look in food merchandising. The motto of the new affluent consumer is "have money, will spend—so go ahead and tempt me"—a heaven-sent answer to the problem of how to enlarge the human stomach. Mrs. High Income may not actually eat more, but she is a delicate creature living on standing rib roast and cantaloupe, and has a grocery bill to match. She is the biggest buyer of many high-margin items—frozen foods, butter, ice cream, beer and wine, dried fruit, paper products, pet foods, snacks and desserts, soft drinks, gourmet foods, and miscellaneous groceries such as condiments and spices. She is also a big buyer of produce and high quality meats.[29]

To captivate Mrs. High Income, and after her Mrs. Newlywed and Mrs. Middle Income, some food retailers have given selected stores the full-scale, film star treatment. Scattered around the country connoisseurs can find stores in Japanese, early American, New Orleans, ranch, riverboat, or nautical styles; the Roman forum, the Hollywood store, the New England barn, the Hacienda, the "Wizard of Id," and the Camelot food palace. No expense has been spared in their design and execution; occasionally they are even furnished with genuine antiques or high class reproductions.

Decor notwithstanding, these film star supermarkets share certain economic fundamentals. They proclaim "we only sell the best," and indeed often do. Their layout has been modified to make sure Mrs. High Income finds it easy to get what she wants, particularly if it carries a high margin. She will get the most service the modern supermarket has to offer, even telephone ordering and home delivery. Naturally the whole package is more expensive. The store makes it up by charging a cent or two more on each item, by the absence of specials and trading stamps, or, more usually, by compensatory profits from high-margin items.

As bait for Mrs. Middle Income and everyone else the food industry is now offering the "Biggest Store in the World" and the "Store with Low Prices." A prototype of the former is the Schwegmann Bros. Giant Supermarket in New Orleans, which has 255,000 sq. ft. (over ten times the size of the average supermarket), with 39 checkstands, and gross sales of $25 million for the year 1965. More modest versions include Giant Foods store in Nashville, Tenn. (60,000 sq. ft.) and Red Owl, in Brookdale, Minn. (32,500 sq. ft.), which is modeled on a "huge, squashed hamburger bun."[30]

These stores are attempting to offer something ambitious in one-stop shopping. They have separate departments selling liquor, delicatessen foods, stationery, paperbacks and greeting cards, plants, drugs and toiletries, snacks and meals, and even clothing.

Average size supermarkets are also doing the same thing though the departments tend not to be so well differentiated. A family flavor is added by carefully geared promotions, bulletin boards with family and community news or recipes, restrooms, and an occasional kiddie korral.

A growing minority have gone into discount operations, and by cutting labor costs and other services are offering a slightly lower priced alternative to conventional shopping. A few are experimenting with a return to the gutted warehouse look of the early thirties, operating on a shoestring and selling by the case-lot at a little above wholesale prices. Another approach is the "convenience" or bantam market, a more businesslike mini-version of the mom and pop store, which stays open long hours, and offers a limited range of merchandise at slightly higher prices.

How, exactly, is the consumer benefiting from all this? Colston E. Warne, president of Consumers Union says, "We have moved full range from a small-scale, inefficient food distribution system to a large-scale and highly costly one. The supermarket of today has not brought a decrease in total distribution costs. Moreover, it has transferred many of the costs of retailing squarely onto the shoulders of the consumer who now pays an ever mounting retail margin for only a fragment of the service he used to get."[31]

As the latest, gaudiest phase of our present "wheel of retailing" runs out, design and decor as a competitive weapon may end in stalemate. When *every* store is handsome, or when the Japanese tea garden is checkmated by the early Colonial supermarket next door, what gimmick will the industry come up with then?

Promotions, selling devices, services, and scientifically designed layouts also cancel each other as soon as everybody uses them. And, as the NCFM pointed out, they are "not easily rescinded for two reasons. They are often physically built into the store and/or are so spectacular that they would be missed by customers."[32] Stores do not like to rip out the air conditioning when times get hard; and check cashing, for example, which most supermarkets do free, costs about 7¢ a check for store handling charges, bank charges, the interest on the money needed to cash them, and bad check losses.[33] This 7¢ simply gets passed on to the shopper, along with the bill for the other fixtures and fittings.

Today's consumer is also getting a very mixed blessing in terms of her shopping experience. At first glance she is the clear winner in the supermarket race to remodel and upgrade. The flip side of the coin, unfortunately, is increasing confusion over prices and creeping manipulation, which make rational shopping harassing, if not impossible. Price juggling makes it extremely difficult to know what any "regular" or "market" price is.

Stores' pricing practices also consistently interfere with the traditional working of supply and demand, which in theory sets prices. Detailed studies of retail prices show that they follow wholesale fluctuations only in a general way, and reflect major trends rather than day-to-day changes. While this can help the consumer when stores decide to hold prices steady, as they did for several months in 1967, it also lessens her traditional leverage over supply and demand. For example, if beef is consistently on special, producers may get inappropriate signals to raise more beef. If they do so, it would not find a market at the "regular" price, and cause a cutback in production, and so on.

For women who want to shop rationally—and there are many who *think* they do, even if the motivation experts might disagree with them—today's supermarket has many elements of a game in which they are trapped by not being told the rules. It makes nonsense of the theoretically alert, informed buyer confronting the honest seller in the marketplace.

The food industry does not want women to shop rationally. If they did, they would be less likely to spend on impulse, or to be affected by the merchandising strategies. Despite industry insistence on giving the customer what she wants, she will be more or less overtly manipulated to change her desires or habits if they become too costly or inconvenient. Most supermarkets would like women to shop evenly throughout the week instead of on weekends, and are currently experimenting with double stamps and specials early in the week. Supermarkets would like to be able to sell frozen meat, rather than (or as well as) fresh, in order to centralize cutting and reduce spoilage; but early attempts to get the housewife to buy it proved a failure. A growing number, now 57.5 percent, are also pushing the idea of prepackaged produce for the same reasons, though many women positively loathe the idea. In a few years' time we can look forward to being conditioned into accepting the "teleshop," or the automated store, a joyless prospect, to say the least.

One price paid by the industry for its marketing techniques, is the general public's noticeable lack of confidence, which became evident during the boycotts. Not understanding the stores' pricing policies, women naturally flared up at the bread and milk price increases of 1966. Fooled by the lush-looking decor and promotional hoopla, they concluded that the stores were making money at their expense. Since then, the industry has taken a new and harder look at its customers. It is, however, a sad commentary on the whole system that to "tell it like it is" would be to give the game away.

Six

THE TRUTH ABOUT PACKAGING

To shop rationally, the housewife would need the impulses of a sleuth, the stamina of a weight-lifter, and the skill of a certified public accountant.

A. Q. MOWBRAY
The Thumb on the Scale

On October 4, 1966, the cartoonist Herblock celebrated the passage of the Fair Packaging and Labeling Act with a drawing which showed an irate consumer shaking a cereal box labeled "New Congressional House Size Super Shredded Truth in Packaging Bill, Fortified with Genuine Hot Air." As four miserable flakes fell out, the consumer asked his hangdog congressman, "This is supposed to serve 200,000,000?"

FPLA was the consumer pyrrhic victory of the decade. Thanks to persistent and strident lobbying by a large number of food and other industry groups,[*1] the act was a weak compromise, lacking the power to protect shoppers from confusion and deception and to see that they got sufficient information to shop rationally. The first to go was a clause which would have made manufacturers list *all* the ingredients on the label. Next was the federal government's right to compel the standardization of package sizes for those product categories that especially perplexed shoppers. What remained was a shamefaced labeling law which made only a mouse-sized dent in the status quo. Manufacturers had to print their name and address and display the net weight prominently, both in ounces and in fractions of pounds, pints, and quarts, etc. They had to define a serving, if these were listed, and drop misleading weight descriptions such as giant and jumbo.

Not only was FPLA feeble, it was wretchedly enforced. Congress was too mean, or too bored with the subject after five years of hearings, to vote sufficient funds, and its enforcement was parceled out among three different federal agencies. The Food and Drug Administration was responsible for food, drugs, and cosmetics; the Federal Trade Commission for other consumer products; and the Office of Weights and Measures in the Commerce Department's Bureau of Standards was asked to obtain voluntary agreement among manufacturers to reduce the number of package sizes.

In fiscal 1968, when Congressional funding was at its most generous, these three agencies were given only an extra $1.08 million among them to finance sixty-two extra staff. By fiscal 1969, the FDA's $115,300 pittance had been slashed in half; the next year it was deleted entirely, leaving the agency with no resources to police the $100 billion food industry, quite apart from the drug and cosmetics manufacturers.

Poor and understaffed, the enforcing agencies appealed to the states for help, yet were unable to offer either a strong policy lead or financial help. One year after FPLA was supposed to be in effect (July 1968) the chief weights and measures official in Washington state summed up local opinion when he said, "Frankly, we are not doing anything until we get some guidelines."[2] In 1969 the states were complaining with a vengeance. "If the Feds want our assistance they should give us a grant for three or four inspectors."

"There must be some methods of educating consumers concerning FPLA; a nation-wide information program. Yet I was told that the FDA and FTC have no information plans." "Confused. I have not been contacted."[3] By October 1969, only ten states had brought their weights and measures laws in line with FPLA, thus assuming the full enforcement burden.

Robbed of their police powers, the federal agents were also hit by the very industries which had stunted FPLA on the vine. Feeble as FPLA was, they still did not want to comply with it, and initiated lawsuits to establish exemptions. The FTC was so bludgeoned it exempted fourteen consumer commodities, ranging from shoelaces to home appliances, primarily to halt the legal proceedings that threatened to stall FPLA till the day of judgment. It also postponed compliance until September 1969. The FDA, which was having similar problems, exempted the following commodities from all or part of the regulations: soft drinks, milk, ice cream, cream, butter, margarine, wheat flour, corn flour, eggs in cartons, all random weight packages, and penny candy.[4] In a few states the baking industry did not even bother to apply for an exemption; it simply made no effort to conform.

By the end of 1969, FDA Commissioner Herbert L. Ley, Jr., "guesstimated" that 70 percent of packages were in line with the new law, though he admitted he did not know for sure. No progress had been made in coming to grips with cents-off offers. The FDA and FTC were still mulling over the problem, as they had been doing for more than four years. There was little reduction in the 8,000 or so items packing the supermarket shelves—though the Commerce Department had haggled well enough to remove 267 package sizes in 25 staples.*[5] A few of these reductions were spectacular, such as toothpaste, down from 57 sizes to 5, but 16 sizes of breakfast cereals and 56 sizes of crackers and cookies were still available.

For the ordinary shopper, FPLA might never have been passed. Grocery shopping is as much of a muddle as ever. Even the most careful, who can ignore advertising, spurn stamps, and are determined to save money, still find themselves playing blindman's buff among packages that make price comparisons and an accurate evaluation of the contents almost impossible.

The core of the trouble is the partial but calculated disappearance of "good old American sizes." Today, only fresh meat, dairy products, margarine, fresh produce (unless sold by the piece), and certain grocery staples, such as sugar, flour, and salad dressing, are commonly sold in full pounds, pints, gallons, or regular fractions thereof. Probably some 60 percent of all food and household products come in non-standard amounts.

One reason is that different products made by the same company are packed in the same size containers, and their net weights vary with their specific gravities. Mostly this is due to economy; it is cheaper to standardize the package than the weight of the contents. Sometimes housewives like it that way. Harrison F. Dunning, president of the Scott Paper Co., explained at the FPLA hearings: "The housewife wants a neat little rack of six kinds of spices and she wants them to look good in her kitchen, so she wants them all the same size. They have different specific gravities, so to fill the bottle you have got to have 2¼ oz. of one, 3½ oz. of another, 4⅛ oz. of a third."

Mr. Dunning's point is not, of course, true for all food products. Manufacturers of dry groceries have considerable latitude over how full they fill the package. With a little less air in the crackers, breakfast cereals, and potato chips industry could hit the full pound target at least *some* of the time.

Allied to the fractional ounce has been a slippage in quantity, concealed by the fact that the price and the container size remain the same. Here are some examples collected during the FPLA hearings by the Hyde Park Co-op (Chicago), the Greenbelt Co-op (Washington D.C.), the Berkeley Consumers Co-op, and Consumers Union:

Product	Old size	New size
Two layer devil food cake mix	20 oz.	19 oz.
Plain angel food cake mix	17 oz.	15 oz.
Pickles	15 oz.	13¾ oz.
Baby food	5 oz.	4¾ and 4½ oz.
Peanut butter	13 oz.	12 oz.
Cake flour	32 oz.	24 oz.
Frozen vegetables	16 oz.	12, 10, 9 then 8 oz.
Fruit flavored drink	64 fl. oz.	57 fl. oz.
Dog food	16 oz.	15½, 15 and 14 oz.
Chocolate-coated graham crackers	16 oz.	14 oz.
Beer	12 oz.	11 oz.
Wheat Chex	18 oz.	14½ oz.
Corn Chex	9 oz.	8 oz.
Life cereal	15 oz.	10 oz.
Chex Mates	9 oz.	7½ oz.
Shredded Wheat	12 oz.	11 oz.
Cream of rice	17½ oz.	16 oz.

In the case of the breakfast cereals, the changes took place between March and April 1965. The slippage is still going on. In May 1969, the House Special Studies subcommittee, headed by Congressman Benjamin S. Rosenthal (D–N.Y.) turned up 600 food and drug items which had dwindled since 1965 without an equivalent decrease in price.

In defending this practice—technically known as packaging to price—the industry uses two arguments, one completely phoney and the other a fascinating insight into how large-scale robbery can be done with slide-rule precision.

The first says that sizes are produced in response to customer demand. Why, inquired Senator Philip A. Hart, (D–Mich.) and others during the FPLA hearings, should Madam prefer 14 oz. or 12 oz. of cookies instead of a full lb.? We are not entirely sure, replied industry witnesses, adding bravely, but we believe that she does. Madam herself was quite emphatic on the point. As one woman put it, "12 oz. of cookies doesn't mean much to me, but the size of the box does. Boy, was I fooled!"[6] During the first two years of the FPLA hearings (1961–63), hundreds of similarly irate shoppers wrote to Consumers Union about these and other packaging tricks, making this the hottest topic in the CU mailbag.

The real reason for tinkering with the net weight is either to make a fast buck, or to recover the rising cost of the raw materials. A classic example of this is the nickel Hershey bar, which varied, until its death from attrition in 1969, from 1½ to 2 oz., depending on the wholesale price of chocolate, but did not sell for more than 5¢ because it is mechanically awkward and psychologically unsound to charge 6¢ or 7¢ for an impulse bar of candy.

For most products the process goes only one way—down. The price rise is concealed, and people either fail to spot it or can do nothing about it because they are never given the choice of paying more money or getting less product. The few cents they lose adds up to millions of dollars for industry. Interestingly enough, it is a form of petty chiseling that goes on at all levels. Raw materials suppliers may try it on their manufacturers, and producers of store brands try it on the chains—if they can get away with it. Where the public is concerned, everyone is home and dry. Once one company starts the slippage, competitors are forced to follow suit.

As if this were not enough, shoppers also have to contend with other favorite marketing stratagems. One is multiple pricing. Another is cents-off, a promise which the manufacturer cannot be sure of keeping, since he cannot dictate the retail price, and which can fool the housewife if she does not know what the "regular" price is. When the free toy, decanter, or hand towel is added to the bag of tricks, rational price comparison becomes practically impossible.

Or does it? One food trade press editor insisted: "My kid is in the seventh grade and she can do it."[7] Grown women, however, could not cope with all the calculation involved. In 1962, Mrs. Helen E. Nelson, then California Consumer Counsel, gave five housewives $10 each, and asked them to buy 14 common food and household

● The food industry's idealized shopper is a prowling computer, jungle-trained, her senses razor-sharp for the sound of a dropping price. In reality she is more likely to be a hummingbird, flitting blindly in a maze of bright packages and confusing displays. She is distracted by supermarket layout, her husband's sweet tooth, and her children's raids on the candy, toys, and snap, crackle, and pop.

items, choosing solely on the basis of the biggest quantity for the lowest price.[8] In 1966, Dr. Monroe Friedman, assistant professor of psychology at Eastern Michigan University, did a similar study with 33 housewives.[9] Two years later, Consumers Union duplicated Mrs. Nelson's test.[10] All the findings were remarkably consistent: Half the time the women could not do what they were asked and purchased a more expensive product. How well will the ordinary shopper fare, who is less on her mettle, pushed for time, and often distracted by her children?

While no one knows how much of the national food money is thereby going down the drain, a few people have hazarded a guess. Senator Hart reckoned $250 a year for a family of four. Professor Friedman said $4.5 billion, or $90 for the same family, and Jerry Voorhis, former executive director of the Cooperative League of the U.S.A. thought $100 million ($2 per family). Any way you look at it, it is too much.

Needless to say the food industry has consistently faulted this type of analysis, arguing that most women do not buy by price, or if they do, have no trouble in figuring it out. During the FPLA hearings a marvelously schizophrenic portrait appeared. Wearing one hat, our prowling computer could detect a bargain with complete accuracy. Wearing another (and there is little doubt which the industry preferred) she shopped like a hummingbird, propelled by psychological satisfaction, the lure of a brand name, or the brightness of a well designed package, which would then fall plop into her shopping cart.

Probably most of us use both shopping styles from time to time, even on the same trip. More might buy like computers if it were not so difficult and time consuming. We should not, however, be denied the information. This is particularly important for the 25.4 million people who live in poverty, and the millions more who are worried about money, all of whom have to skimp on food to varying degrees and who need help to make price comparisons *easily*.

It is a fundamental principal of our free enterprise system that consumers be given enough information to shop intelligently—and food packages should be no exception. What use, for example, is the net weight if we are not told how much of it is air, ice, or water? Two cans recently opened by the author illustrate the problem. One 8 oz. can of Dutch fancy whole onions, said to serve 2–3 people, whose label showed a dish of 17 onions, in fact held eight, weighing 4 oz., swimming in 4 oz. of brine. A 1 lb. can of Wilson's Tender Made Ham housed 9½ oz. of meat, 2½ oz. of fat, and 4 oz. of water and gelatin, a mixture which raised the price of the edible meat to $1.66 a lb. Neither container stated the net drained weight. During the five years of the FPLA hearings a large number of similar cases were cited, amid small screams of rage by consumers who resented deception and the resulting loss of faith.

A related problem is slack fill, or as *Mad* magazine neatly put it, "a lot of paper at cookie prices." Justified by industry as the mechanical need to cushion fragile products against breakage, to allow for settling during shipment, and to provide headspace during canning, this device has tended to become another dubious race for profits. Its all-time leader is the manufacturer of Delson Thin Mints, whose product was seized by the FDA because it filled a mere 45 percent of the actual and 75 percent of the practical volume of the container.[11] The agency met its Vietnam, since the courts upheld Delson's explanation that their breakable mints required this amount of protective cushioning. Other mint makers, some of whom testified that they had been getting on very well without such protection, rushed to adjust their packaging. And the FDA is powerless to do much about them, or about the cracker, cookie, potato chip, detergent, and breakfast cereal brigades, some of whom have been known to be 12-48 percent short. Though it has discretionary authority under FLPA to regulate "non-functional" slack fill, it has no funds to do so, and national standards exist only for some canned fruit and vegetables. Some states have the power to set up their own standards, but few have done so, for the simple reason that they could not be enforced.

Even if the housewife knew exactly how much was in the package, and at what price, she would often be in the dark about quality. She can be misled by the brilliance of food industry graphics, e.g., the glossy TV dinner boxes, and certain cans of fruit and vegetables, which are a good deal more attractive than their contents. More serious is a lack of basic nutritional information. Only pet food packages list *all* the ingredients in the proportions they appear; this was done by manufacturers to lure dog and cat owners away from the older, thriftier habit of feeding table scraps. Humans are not so lucky.

Ingredients in the some 380 products for which there are FDA or other standards of identity are published in the Code of Federal Regulations (titles 7, 9, and 21). For some reason the FDA standards do not appear on the package. Possibly in the "good old days" when housewives made their own jam and mayonnaise they knew what went into them. Today, food technology is so much more complicated (and so few women make jam) that hardly anyone knows.

Processed meat and poultry products are regulated by the USDA, which sets limits on the amount of extenders which may be used, and minimum standards for the meat content. Some processed fish is covered by the U.S. Department of the Interior, which sets minimum ratios of fish to batter and breadcrumbs. Here—and in all other foods—the ingredients are listed on the label in the order of predominance, beginning with the largest. Without the percentages, however, nobody is much wiser. Manufacturers claim that to reveal percentages would divulge trade secrets. In the overwhelming majority of cases, this is not true. Competitors know what goes into the other fellow's can, though they may not know the sequence, the blending techniques, or certain of the additives or flavorings.

But how can consumers know the precise difference between processed and natural cheese, between ice milk and ice cream, and which is the most nutritious product? (See Appendix 11.) How many realize that many prepared meat, fish, and poultry items have less of the name product than they imagine, and that differences in terminology are not copywriters' whimsy but an index of meatability? Here are some examples:

Product	Minimum percent meat
Lightly breaded shrimp	65%
Frozen breaded raw shrimp	50
Chile con carne	40
Chile con carne with beans	25
Spaghetti with meat balls and sauce	12
Spaghetti with sauce and meat balls	6
Boned canned chicken	90–95
Boned canned chicken with broth	80
Strained chopped chicken with broth	43
Chicken dinnners	18 (or a minimum 2 oz.)

It would probably come as an unpleasant surprise to people who buy franks under the assumption that they are nutritious and contain no waste, that they can contain up to 10 percent water, 3½ percent extender (unless they state "all meat"), and 30 percent fat, i.e., nearly 45 percent junk and the rest substandard meat.

Millions of people who are watching their weight, who are on low- or no sodium diets, who have food allergies, or who merely wish to avoid as many additives as possible get little help from the label, since many of these ingredients are either not required to be listed or are lumped under a blanket description like "seasonings" or "preservatives." At a time when we are extremely concerned about nutrition and the effects of diet and chemicals on health, we are prevented from finding out from food packages what to eat and what to avoid by the food industry's insistence that its profits are more important than the public welfare.

As a crowning touch to our ignorance, we cannot even be sure if what is inside the package is fresh, or, in the case of perishables, how long it can safely be kept. Where preservation-laden groceries are concerned, this question is academic, but in the case of processed meats, bacon, dairy products, and cream cakes a cutoff eating date would be a big help. Such information is provided in certain Scandinavian countries, and in Britian by the redoubtable Marks & Spencer Ltd. (see Chap. 7), but not in this country, largely because manufacturers fear that women will rumple their shelf displays searching for the freshest items. In fact, most packaged foods and some fresh meats have a concealed code on them, either pinpointing the date, time, and place of manufacture, or the date when they should be pulled from the shelves by the manufacturer's representative. Each firm has its own code; to the public they are as helpful as an Egyptian hieroglyph. But on occasions they have been deciphered.

An attractive housewife, Marguerite Kelly, using brains and determination, persuaded five major chains in the Washington, D. C., area to decipher the codes, particularly the pull dates, on their meat, eggs, and dairy products. Unfortunately, she found no simple formula, no Rosetta Stone, which could be used elsewhere. She also anticipated that everything would be changed after the *Washington Post* published her story.[12]

It will not surprise anyone who reads this dismal chronicle that further packaging reform is long overdue. The most obvious aid to rational shopping would be unit pricing, i.e., the price per ounce or pound marked on either the shelf or the label, as is now the case with fresh meat, fish, poultry, and cheese. At the time of writing (October 1969) a number of amendments to FPLA had been introduced. Some would require unit pricing, and one (HR 14816) would require the pull-dating of perishable foods.[13]

More to the point, some local experiments are being tried which may overcome stores' reluctance to add to their operating costs for a doubtful sales return. At the request of Congressman Benjamin S. Rosenthal (D–N.Y.), a two-month test run of dual pricing began in September 1969 in two Washington, D.C., Safeway stores.[14] In one store, prices were marked on the shelves; in the other, customers were supplied with mini slide-rule computers, latched to the shopping carts, and were instructed how to do their own calculations.[15]

In New York City, a law requiring unit pricing was pushed through following hearings conducted by Bess Myerson Grant, head of the Department of Consumer Affairs. The first phase, covering half of food store volume, went into effect in February 1970. Stores are required to mark packages with the unit price as well as the total price, or post the unit price on the shelf or in a list displayed at the end of the aisle.

Ultimately unit pricing will probably be adopted because it will allow manufacturers to go on playing the packaging to price game while giving Madam a better idea of what they are doing. She will of course, pay for this information with higher food prices. New York City retailers are already moaning that unit pricing will set them back $50 million a year,[16] while Clarence Adamy, president of the National Association of Food Chains, estimated that the overall cost would be $300 million.[17] As usual, industry gets us into a jam, then hands us the bill for our own rescue! The alternative, which manufactureres would like less, would be to go back to the "good old American sizes," raising prices when necessary in a good honest fashion.

Persuading (or forcing) the trade to add more information to its labels is likely to be more difficult. Packaging is so vital a weapon in the battle of the supermarket that industry will not tolerate more than a minimum of federal regulation. The package, "the world's greatest mobile billboard," is the passport to a place on the increasingly crowded shelves. It is the only way in which the manufacturer can catch Madam's eye today, when so much shopping is done on impulse. Designers have calculated that it takes her a mere four seconds to scan the sales area where a particular product may be found. In that twinkling of an eye the battle for her sales dollar is either won or lost. Packaging is also an addition to advertising for the famous national brands, and a substitute for it by small competitors who can hope to out-package but not out-advertise the giants. It is the breath of life for breakfast cereal manufacturers, whose main hope of sales is to keep the attention of the school age generation.

With more undifferentiated products on the market, packaging accentuates the brand image and persuades the shopper to buy brand A instead of brand B. Many firms whose sales or image were sagging, or whose new products were in a declining phase of their life cycle, have redesigned their packaging with gratifying results.*[18] Many a firm that wished to break into or keep its place in a crowded market has come out with a gimmick package —a plastic toy, a pitcher, or a dimpled bottle—and scored heavily at the cash register.[19]

Any new attempt to change the labeling regulations or enforce the now voluntary standardization of sizes will drag out the objections aired at the FPLA hearings. The first will be the Albania argument. It is fine for industry to tinker with packaging, but let Uncle Sam try it and the result will be drabness, uniformity, stifled initiative, and (the ultimate threat) fewer new products. The second argument will be expense. Redesign is very, very expensive, and the cost will as usual be passed on to the consumer.

The truth is that neither of these points is really valid. Manufacturers can perfectly well standardize some of their sizes. They have already done so in the case of liquor, milk, butter, flour, lard, margarine, shortening, regular coffee, and even can sizes, which have come down over the years from 200 to about 32. They are doing so now under the Department of Commerce, which could get better and faster results with more money and an extension of its authority under FPLA. As for blighting the supermarket, a reduction in the number of items would allow the survivors to shine more brightly. Chains would be able to offer more *variety* by stocking more brands. Alternatively they might decide to reduce the sales areas in stores not yet built, thus lowering their operating costs. As for being deprived of new products, what would we be missing?

While redesigning a package is unquestionably expensive (see Appendix 8), it would cost less for the manufacturers to do so for Uncle Sam than as part of the daily business round. Containers are changed when the sales situation demands it—and the present food industry treadmill is demanding it increasingly often—whereas the government could wait until existing label or package stocks had run out. A survey by Benson & Benson Inc. showed that half the responding companies had altered their packages in the past five years, and 45 percent were contemplating the purchase of new packaging machinery.[20] One packaging trade association spokesman told the FPLA hearings, "Changes can occur virtually overnight. Once something more appealing is offered to customers, and they respond favorably by buying the product in the new package rather than the old, every other manufacturer is forced to offer the consumer some type of improvement." If the product flops, the money is wasted. Either way, the cost is passed on to the public.

This vicious competitive climate is one reason that the national packaging bill is so high. In 1968 we spent $31.9 billion— equivalent to two-fifths of what we spend on defense, three-quarters of what we spend on education, and more than three times the bill for welfare.[21] Containers for food and beverages accounted for 56 percent of this sum, i.e., $357 for a family of four. It should be self-evident that we have a right to see that this money is better spent.

A number of reforms are in the air which industry ought to be able to live with. The first is that packages should list all the nutritional ingredients in the percentages in which they appear. Such a list would have to include "water" or "moisture," which hardly falls under the nutritional heading, but is so ubiquitous that it could not be omitted without causing gross deception.

Many consumers would like to know the net drained weight, where relevant, plus a list of all additives used in the processing. Here, unfortunately, there would be severe technical problems. Many canned fruits, for example, absorb moisture during the first two or three months, so that any statement of their net drained weight would have to be very approximate and might not be helpful. Listing *all* the additives would put many chains, whose private label manufacturing is done by several companies, in a real dilemma. A single product often comes from more than one supplier; the ordering chain often does not know what additives (or even what type of syrup or shortening) will turn up in different batches. Even if a complete list could be found it would create tremendous pressures on label space. Small products like chewing gum would have to be packed in envelopes; the type size on many others would shrink to the size of the proverbial Lord's Prayer on a grain of rice. Since a few additives are so obscure as to perplex even food chemists, would consumers be much the wiser? Again, a compromise could be arranged. Salt at least should be listed for the benefit of slimmers, and the FDA should keep an open mind about requiring that additives, or even actual foods, such as corn products, be listed if they prove to be common causes of allergy.

Implementation of one or more of these ideas is by no means unrealistic. Many consumer groups, disgusted by the FPLA fiasco, are pressing for them, as are some congressmen (e.g., members of the Democratic Study Group Task Force) and the prestigious White House Conference on Food, Nutrition and Health, which met in December 1969. Even the FDA is beginning to wonder whether its standards at least should not appear on the package. More political pressures from ordinary shoppers could well be the clincher. If industry could be persuaded that the housewife really preferred to be a prowling computer, it might give in more gracefully.

$\mathcal{S}$even

THE SUPERMARKET UNDERWORLD

A great many apparently law-abiding citizens are overcome with a yet to be understood urge to get something for nothing and steal things from self-service stores.

ROGER K. GRIFFIN
Assistant general manager,
Commercial Service Systems Inc.,
The Shoplifter: Shadow or Substance?

M rs. X, wife of a police officer, was caught with $7.94 worth of merchandise hidden in her purse, a bonus on her paid weekly order of $43.62. After making the usual remorseful noises ("I don't know what came over me"), she confessed to have taken $113 worth of goods in previous weeks. Later it was discovered that her mother, likewise a police officer's wife, with whom she regularly went shopping, had also been caught in the act a little while before.[1]

Deep in the files of the Food and Drug Administration is another case, this time of a nimble- rather than a light-fingered lady, who was found stealing in a different way. She was employed by a Wisconsin factory to help in the production of phoney Swiss cheese, 2,700 lbs. of which had just been seized at the instigation of an FDA inspector. Her job was to gouge "eyes" in cheap "blind swiss" cheese with a melon scoop, so that it could sell at a higher "bargain" price.[2]

These two cases illustrate what goes on in the supermarket underworld of buyers vs. sellers, and vice versa. It is a gray area characterized by dishonesty, suspicion, carelessness, and protestations, and reinforced by an unclear or unhelpful legal system. It spawns pilferage, robbery, vandalism, cartnapping, and rubber checks—and on the industry side, short-weighting, deceptive advertising, overcharging, and tampering with product quality. It also adds to the food bill, creating a situation where the last laugh is at the expense of the honest shopper.

Every day U.S. retailers arrest 6,000 to 8,000 people for shoplifting, an offense which has doubled since 1960. The average supermarket detects 8.7 cases a week[3] but estimates that another 17 people get away. It is impossible to get accurate figures on the take, simply because there are many factors that cause "inventory shrink," and hardly any of the stores keep detailed records on precisely how much was stolen, dropped, spoiled, or not delivered. However, the industry estimates that total supermarket losses due to pilferage are between $300 and $850 million a year.[4] For the average store, this is at least $28,000 a year.

"Shoplifters are not sick people," said the industry magazine *Supermarketing* (formerly *Food Topics*.) "They are average, everyday, run-of-the-mill segments of our population. They are Mr. and Mrs. America and their kids."[5]

Shoplifting is not related to poverty. It goes on in all types of neighborhoods and most of the people who are discovered have enough cash on them to pay for what they stole. A man in Berkeley, California, was caught appropriating two 45¢ bars of imported chocolate, while carrying the unbelievable sum of $1,100. Nobody knows exactly why they do it, though theories come as thick as cents-off offers, ranging from a contempt for the establishment, the search for kicks, doing it for dares, and the usual moralistic notions that we have abandoned our belief in God, "the greatest security control that ever existed." A hard core steal simply to make money or to support their drug habit.

The most favored items are non-foods,[6] particularly cigarettes, liquor, health and beauty aids, nylons, candy, gum, and razor blades; canned meats and delicatessen items are also popular. These products are the easiest to sell. Ironically for the industry, which tries so hard to tempt the shopper, they are also impulse items. Fresh meat is also a common traget, particularly steak, which is expensive and fits snugly under the armpit.

The corniest ways of stealing are still the commonest. Women stuff goodies into their purses or under the baby, and both sexes load their clothing, particularly their pockets. Other methods are slightly more imaginative; people tuck nylons, phonograph records, and steaks into newspapers or magazines. They add to the contents of their berry box, transfer butter into margarine containers, stuff toothbrushes down rolls of paper towels, switch bottle tops, and change the tags on meat packages to get away with roasts at hamburger prices. A few mothers load their young children with packages and send them to wait outside while they go through the checkstand in the usual way. Others get through with merchandise piled on the lower rack of the cart.

The pro, not content with the $3.40 worth that amateurs normally take, uses a few special tricks. A favorite is still the "booster box" in one of its different forms. Usually this is a box either plastered with the name of another store, or sealed and addressed as if for mailing, which has a false bottom into which pilfered items are slipped. Sometimes it is merely a bag which is filled, then stapled shut over a phoney receipt. Another variation is a regular brown supermarket sack, which is piled with the target items and parked, still in the cart, near one of the store exits. The thief then wanders off, selects a few other things, and pays for them at the checkout. On the way out he collects the cart, with its illicit cargo, and vanishes to the limbo of the parking lot.

Other loners use a bulky overcoat, with extra deep pockets, with or without belts or hooks on which to attach the loot. A few women use the "crotch method," having toned their leg muscles so that they can walk, or waddle, out with supplies of coffee or large canned hams between their thighs.

Some pros team up, often concentrating on duping the checkout clerk, either by distracting her and sneaking items through, or by tricking her into giving extra change. In a "duplicate shop," thief number one buys a load of stuff, then hands his cash register tape to number two, who selects identical items and walks out without paying for them.

Armed robbery is on the increase. During 1966, 4,600 chain stores of all kinds were robbed at the checkout. Because of the large amounts of cash and checks on hand, supermarkets are the biggest single category of business to be hit, especially in urban areas. In the same year, 5,400 food and other retailers were also burgled *each week*, most often at opening or closing time, with total losses of $70 million. More grocers are getting shot on the job. Consequently, they are clamoring for extra police protection and learning how to shoot back.

Other ugly forms of violent or organized crime are hitting the industry, Hijacking trucks carrying food (especially meat) and other items have become so common that in 1969 the American Trucking Association formed the Trucking Industry Committee on Thievery and Hijacking (TICOTH) to try to cope with it. The Mafia, too, have a foothold in the food industry, centering on New York and New Jersey. In 1964 they did $50 million worth of arson damage to A & P, as well as killing two managers, to "persuade" that firm to stock a detergent in which Cosa Nostra had an interest.[7] In New York, a special State Investigation Commission found that consumers there were paying higher food prices for Mafia controlled meat, bananas, and bagels, and to foot the bill for loans and extortions extracted from the merchants.[8]

Quite apart from actual stealing, customers manage to destroy a good deal of merchandise through carelessness. There is Peggy the Poker, who manhandles a good deal of meat and produce before buying it, gets frustrated by packages in general, or only wants one

of something, and rips them open. There is the shopper with but-
terfingers, who knocks bottles off the shelves or breaks something
as she unloads her cart at the checkstand, and the child who is
trying to help but cannot quite make it. Another pest is the shopper
who decides *not* to buy something after she has it in her cart, or
finds she has run out of money. She will dump a package on the
floor, frozen peas in the produce department, or ice cream in the
appetizers. As a result food spoils, the store looks like the after-
math of a ball game, and a clerk often has to be specially assigned
to scurry around after misplaced merchandise. This problem is
particularly acute in poverty areas, but it also goes on in the suburbs where shoppers might be expected to be more careful.

Other people eat up supermarket profits more literally, a habit
the industry calls "grazing." They swig cola, munch fruit, shell
peanuts, pacify the kids with Crackerjack, discard the half-eaten
remainder, and then forget to pay for it, or, with an ingenuous
smile hand the clerk an apple core to be weighed with their purchases. As a customer interpretation of self-service it is not without its humorous side, but it is not funny for the store, which has
to sell $5 worth of merchandise to recoup the cost and profit for
every 5¢ candy bar consumed.

Another problem is cartnapping. One to eight percent of all
supermarket shopping carts are trundled away or are so damaged
as to be useless. Particularly in big cities, where more people walk
to shop, carts are removed to take the goodies home, then wind up
as laundry carriers, flower baskets, frying grills, or scooters. In the
suburbs fewer are taken away, and many are recovered from back
yards and street corners, but more get clobbered in the stores' own
parking lots due to carelessness. Occasionally carts are rounded up
by professional hijackers, who enter the parking lots with a truck,
load up, vanish, and then sell the haul to another supermarket.
Carts are expensive, running anywhere from $25 to $35 each. Annual loss, damage, and pickup services cost the industry up to
$10,000 per supermarket.

Bad checks, too, are an exceedingly costly form of carelessness,

resulting mainly from people's miscalculation of their bank bal-
ances. It is particularly serious for supermarkets, which now cash
$1.1 billion a week in checks, more than banks, hotels, or any
other kind of business.[9] In any week, the average food store
grosses $20,400, cashes checks worth $26,000, and gets ten rubber
checks with an average value of $16.76, out of which thirty-five
will be uncollectable at the year's end. In a few cases the duds are
the result of deliberate fraud; professional "paperhangers" find it
relatively easy to get around stores' check-cashing requirements,
using a whole kit of drivers' licenses and social security cards for
the purpose. Others come from people who are shiftless, poor
credit risks, or fall on hard times and cannot pay up. One way or
another the FBI estimates that supermarkets get hit for almost
40 percent of all bad check losses, some $240 million a year.

It is clear that customers, however desirable in the mass and
charming as individuals, are, on occasion, perfectly awful. Surprisingly, stores' employees can be worse. Here are some examples from security firms' files: the night crew found cooking lobster
in the basement (the firm had been losing gourmet foods); the
maintenance man, who said complacently, "I steal all my groceries
from this store. I also get my meats here"; and the tyrant-manager,
who for years had insisted on opening and closing the store himself, and for years had been walking out with two bags of free
groceries.

Employee theft exceeds that of customers by an estimated two
to one, for a yearly total of $100–$300 million. How many employees are guilty is anyone's guess; firms like to think most of
their staff are honest, else they could not operate, but when they
find out, they are often shocked. One chain ran polygraph tests on
1,400 employees and found that 76 percent of them had stolen
more than $100 in cash or goods during the previous six months.[10]

Many of those caught are tried and true fellows with honest
faces, even noticeably vigilant at spotting customer shoplifting; as
a security officer suggested, it takes one to know one. Others have
grudges against the firm for not promoting them or paying them

enough, or they steal because store morale is low, and the manager sets a bad example by being sloppy in his bookkeeping, or in on the act himself. Others do it because they are constantly exposed to temptation and it is so easy to give in.

There are said to be over 4,000 ways in which employees can walk off with cash, merchandise, or stamps.[11] Much of it goes on at the checkout, where checkers can fail to ring up a sale and pocket the money, or conceal money and stamps in their pockets, smocks, bags, or loose shoes, and decant it during frequent trips to the rest room. Others simply remove merchandise—like the bag-boy who parked his car near the store entrance with the trunk unlocked, and in a few seconds had whipped in $10 worth of cigarettes. Not infrequently thefts are the fruit of mutual cooperation. One night crew was found smuggling out goods via the store's incinerator. A store manager and his assistant siphoned off $75,000 a year via an unscheduled cash register which remained undetected for three years. Perhaps at this very moment, countless "sweetheart cashiers" are ringing up purchases for their friends at a fraction of the true cost.

Vendors, too, are guilty, particularly when stores are careless about recording deliveries. The security officer for the Jewel Co. chain said his firm had observed "hindquarters and other good-size pieces of meat disappearing during the meat delivery or some time after, doubtless to be resold to another store."[12] They had also found the soft drinks man not giving proper credit for cases of empties, and concluded that any vendor might try to cheat if not carefully watched. Added another security chief, "If a store manager doesn't call me up to report at least one vendor shortage during the week, I know that he is not telling everything."[13]

Employees can be just as sloppy and destructive as customers, particularly when morale is low or labor relations bad. It is likely that more than $22 million a year is lost through breakage and damage, plus an additional $13 million for damage in the ware-house or during shipping. Being human, employees make mistakes: They slash the contents while opening cartons with a cutter blade, or drop merchandise while stacking it on the shelves. Like customers, they nibble, snacking through boxes of cookies, candies, fruit, and soda pop; "borrowing" some bread, lunch meat, and mustard to make a sandwich; or even cooking a lunchtime snack in the privacy of the store's back room.

Not surprisingly, supermarket managements are stepping up security arrangements to prevent pilferage and catch offenders, while trying not to give staff or customers the feeling of being spied upon. More stores are using full- or part-time security staff, often off-duty police, to patrol stores during the peak shopping hours, especially in cities and ghettos. More stores are also using commercial security services,[14] both routinely, and to a lesser extent for special loss-measuring assignments. Such firms employ trained investigators who can blend perfectly with shoppers (in pearls or pedal-pushers) to catch shoplifters and to measure checker honesty and courtesy. When employee shoplifting is a particular problem, these firms will supply investigators who pose as staff for a few weeks, chat with their colleagues over a glass of beer, and report on internal security arrangements.

Employees, too, are being trained to keep a sharp but friendly eye on customers. A courteous "Hi!" or "Good morning!" is now part of store policy; it pleases the bona fide customer, and also helps to remind the light-fingered that someone is watching them.

Supplementing these efforts are a variety of gadgets designed to catch shoplifters, and some electronic systems which many stores are toying with but few are using because they are expensive.[15] The simplest is the clear plastic produce bag, which cuts down on attempts to smuggle out other items with the lettuce. Many stores use a one-way mirror, 16"–20" high, set at an angle in the upper wall, which enables someone in the upstairs office to oversee the most vulnerable parts of the store—the health and beauty aids section, the paper aisle, and the meat and delicatessen counters. Next commonest is the plain clothes guard, often disguised as an ordinary shopper.

More sophisticated is the closed-circuit TV system, or dummy TV camera (which works just as well as a deterrent until customers tumble to it), and the two-man team, one posted upstairs behind the mirror, and the second in the store, who communicate by walkie-talkie.

Still newer, and used by only a small number of companies, is an electronic bug the size of a grain of pepper, which is placed on packets of meat, housewares, cosmetics, or cigarettes, and which works in conjunction with a radio transmitter and a scanner. When the item is paid for the dot is neutralized by a deactivator concealed under the checkout. If removed past the checkout, either through malice or forgetfulness, the bug signals the scanner, which triggers a flashing sign over the exit saying "YOU FORGOT TO PAY FOR AN ITEM. EITHER RETURN IT OR PAY FOR IT AT THE CHECKSTAND. IF YOU PROCEED BEYOND THIS POINT AN ALARM WILL SOUND"—in the manager's office.

Coping with armed robbery is a different matter, and stores are still debating whether to arm their managers and teach them how to shoot. On the whole there is a reluctance to use force, partly because many robbers are sick enough to shoot first and desperate enough to kill. Instead, stores are being advised to keep minimum supplies of cash on hand and bank it frequently.

Recovery of shopping carts—lost, stolen, or strayed—is still an unsolved problem. Store managers and staff periodically plod around the neighborhood, roping in the stragglers, sometimes with the help of firms which specialize in this kind of herding, or even neighborhood kids. Other firms swear by "carriage corrals," where carts are unloaded from a sheep-pen arrangement of metal rails and posts, or a magnetic barrier at the parking lot exits which automatically lock the wheels of any carts being removed from the lot. In a few other cases local big city merchants have run joint advertising campaigns, stressing that cartnapping is dirty pool, and that the cost of the carts merely goes on the food bill. They have also stocked little two-wheel shopping carts, which are sold to customers at cost or given free after a specified amount of groceries have been purchased. Such campaigns work well, for a time, and then gradually the carts start rolling away again.

Bad checks are a chronic problem because there is as yet no cheap and universal system for ensuring that the customer actually has money in her account. Limited use is being made of local credit reporting services (supermarkets subscribe to a computer system which has been fed with customers' check cashing history) and check guarantee systems (a commercial company becomes co-maker of the check along with the customer). A few firms are experimenting with credit cards, which are said to be successful in cutting losses and stimulating purchases, despite their cost.[16] Because these methods are expensive, most stores are relying on better identification from customers, placing limits on the amounts of personal checks that can be cashed, or charging a small check-cashing fee, which is often remitted when merchandise is purchased.

Stores are also (reluctantly) getting much tougher with the customer. Every year a slightly higher percentage of apprehended shoplifters are prosecuted (currently 26.7 percent) as stores overcome their fear of losing patrons, making mistakes, or behaving illegally and being sued for false arrest. Judges and district attorneys are also less inclined to view shoplifting as trivial. Unless the offender is old, pregnant, or pitiful, he or she is increasingly likely to wind up in jail or with a fine for the first offense. Light-fingered employees are usually fired, since they are likely to go on stealing, and a good crack of the whip every now and then helps keep the rest of the staff on the straight and narrow.

Aside from these precautions, stores are not without their own offensive tactics against customers. Since time immemorial merchants have had a built-in incentive to short-weight as a quick and easy way to make an extra buck, and supermarkets continue the tradition. According to Leland J. Gordon, Director of the Denison University, Ohio, Weights and Measures Research Center, there are forty-six ways of swindling customers.[17] On a few occasions people get taken for large amounts,[*18] but most shortages are small, probably less than one ounce.

The best opportunity to short-weight is in the packages stores make up themselves, particularly meat. Most sealers of weights and measures complained to Dr. Gordon of widespread shorting; e.g., in Illinois, 80 percent of the stores checked in one city were caught and the damage to the customers on meat alone was around $250,000 a day. A favorite trick is to weigh the product together with its tray or wrapping paper, or not make a complete allowance for the extent to which meat will shrink in one to three days on the counter because of dehydration. Less commonly, stores may try selling meat by the piece; a few years ago an Oklahoma market advertised six pork chops for $1 but omitted to mention that each chop was only the size of a nickel.

A second danger spot is faulty scales, whether accidental or intentional. Dodges in this department include weighing "on the swing," rigging the scale to over-read by a few ounces. One Florida grocer attached an 8 oz. weight to the underside of the scale by a black thread which ran through a tiny hole in the counter to a shelf underneath. Whenever the customer was not looking he slipped the weight off the shelf and let it swing.

When Dr. Gordon asked sealers how much short-weighting they thought was deliberate, half could not say, while the other half guessed between 1 and 10 percent. The sealer from Tennessee said, "Ten percent are never honest, twenty-five percent are as honest as we make them be, and sixty-five percent are honest, but even they have to be alerted and kept conscious of their responsibility."

Another tactic is simple overcharging. The food industry claims that most checkout errors (which can average 100–200 a month per store) are honest mistakes, and half the time favor the customer. There is probably a one in ten chance that housewives will get charged the regular rather than the advertised price for a special.[19] In some cases there is no marked price, in others, there are two or three prices superimposed, and the checker charges the full amount. Stores consistently deny accusations from poverty groups that this is deliberate.

Some store advertising leaves a lot to be desired in terms of honesty and clarity. As every housewife knows, ads do not always mention the size and weight of the advertised items or their original prices. Sometimes specials turn out to be unavailable: A 1969 survey by the FTC[20] found 7 percent out of stock in San Francisco, and 23 percent in Washington, D.C. Whether they were in short supply, sold faster than expected, or were meant as "bait" rather than as a genuine sale is impossible to prove. Other times the customer is left in doubt when the special offer ends, and even if she gets a "raincheck" cannot always find the brand she wants next time.

Such advertising is, of course, perfectly legal. Complaints are rarely made to the Federal Trade Commission, though they do come to local consumer organizations, Better Business Bureaus, departments of weights and measures, and district attorneys. The FTC starts taking an interest only when food industry advertising is obviously false.*[21]

In one agreeable exception to this laissez-faire policy, the FTC started hearings in January 1970 on a new trade regulation that would force retailers to maintain adequate stocks and to sell advertised items at the advertised price.

A second area in which consumers may see some action, at least in Nassau County, New York, is in the mislabeling of meat, specifically the practice of selling cheaper cuts as higher priced ones, such as chuck for round and round for boneless sirloin. In December 1969, Nassau County Executive Eugene H. Nickerson accused 30 stores, including every major chain in the area, of this deception, and claimed that shoppers in the county were probably being bilked of $5 million a year. While it is possible that Mr. Nickerson is in error, or that Nassau County is a hotbed of fraud, it is highly likely that this swindle is widespread and merits investigation.

Another element in the supermarket underworld are food manufacturers who deliberately or accidentally dupe the consumer. Like stores, they have a tendency to short-weight, partly to make a quick buck, but mostly through breakdown of check-weighting arrangements before the goods leave the factory.

A small amount of shorting is caught by the Food and Drug Administration; rather more is caught by state and local sealers of weights and measures in the stores or in the manufacturers' plants, though they are very variable in their enthusiasm and effectiveness.

The most persistent offenders, in the view of many sealers, are bread manufacturers. One Missouri official told Dr. Gordon that "when competition gets rough, bakers reduce the size of the loaf 1–2 oz. In one of our exhibits we had 16, 18 and 20 oz. loaves of bread, all of which had been baked in the same pans."

A number of poultry processors also qualify for the rogues' gallery for selling the consumer H_2O at broiler prices, a commodity technically known as "watered poultry." Here, the chickens absorb more than the legal maximum (8 percent of their dry weight) of the 10 gallons of water and ice in which they are cleaned and packed. In the view of Senator Joseph Montoya (D–N.M.), based on a General Accounting Office survey, such illegal processing was done by 44 firms producing 13 percent of all poultry shipped in interstate commerce during 1967—a practice to which the USDA turned a blind eye.

Many manufacturers contend that short-weighting is caused by mechanical difficulties in always producing the correct weight, and climatic and other factors which can affect the density of a product and the amount of moisture it absorbs. No such excuse, however, can be given for a chronic tendency to tamper with the product: the gradual (legal) reduction of the contents noted by many consumer witnesses at the Truth in Packaging hearings, or the alteration of product ingredients, sometimes legal and sometimes not, which fools the shopper because it is so hard to detect.

Such tampering always involves reducing one or more good, expensive ingredients. Where this happens in the absence of a food

standard, and is gross enough to constitute misrepresentation, the
FDA can seize the offending product on the grounds that it is "mis-
labeled." In recent years the FDA has ordered off the market many
pancake and other syrups where the sorghum, molasses, and maple
has been partially or wholly replaced with cheaper corn syrup; a
consignment of Carnation Instant Breakfast where the natural
sweeteners had been replaced by cyclamates, and a number of
canned and frozen fish products, even a batch of codfish masquer-
ading as frozen devilled crab.

Where products violate an existing FDA or USDA food standard
they can be seized by those agencies on grounds of adulteration.
Foremost Dairies lost 300 cases of Milkman instant dry milk
(heavily advertised in the West as tasting better than milk because
it was made with cream) which contained 7 percent fat instead
of the standard 26 percent. The FDA has caught a number of cases
of watered-down orange juice,*22 ice cream inflated with air, fruit
cocktails and mixed vegetables lacking a small amount of an expensive ingredient, and salad dressings with less than 35 percent
vegetable oil.

Evidence of a considerable amount of adulteration among
processed meats was revealed during the hearings on the 1967 meat
inspection act. State inspectors found hams pumped up with more
than the legal 10 percent of water or laced with chemicals like
sodium nitrate, and sausage with illegal amounts of extender. In
a survey of non-federally inspected meat, the USDA found Safeway,
Piggly-Wiggly, A & P, Kroger, and First National Stores selling
franks and bologna with 2–4 times the legal amount of water or
extender, and pork sausage treated with coloring agents to make
it look fresh. Some of these products had come from Swift and
Armour, two of the largest meat packing firms in the country.*23

On a few occasions, industry-wide swindling results in a gradual
quality slippage which is quite at odds with modern advances in
food technology. Frozen dinners do not contain as much meat as
they used to, and fruit pies do not have as much fruit.24 Cane and
maple syrup is nearly all cane; mayonnaise is often made without

egg yolk; cheaper coffee beans are frequently used in instant coffee; and frankfurters have been absorbing increasing amounts of fat.

If sales are affected, or ethical products start losing ground, the FDA, USDA, USDI, and sometimes even consumers press for a new food standard—an official ingredients list which will restore public confidence and give honest manufacturers a break. One example of this is peanut butter, which the FDA, consumers, and the industry have been hassling over since 1959. There is a tendency to have fewer peanuts and more goop (hydrogenated oils and sweeteners), until many brands had degenerated into what one consumer group called "peanut flavored face-cream."

Alongside this product de-escalation, there is a shady aspect of food companies' advertising, particularly health claims concerning dieting. During recent years the FDA has caught a handful of firms for misrepresenting their product as being low in cholesterol or helping to prevent serious heart disease, e.g., Nabisco (Shredded Wheat) and Kraft (Miracle Egg).

In other instances firms confuse people with nutritional gobble-degook—like the non-dairy cream substitutes, which imply that they are reducing aids, yet may have 20 percent more saturated fatty acids than cream, and are high in cholesterol, thanks to being made with coconut oil; Wonder Bread, original model for the wittier Volkswagen ad with its claim to build strong bodies; "power protein" breakfast cereal which provides less than six percent of the recommended daily protein allowance per serving; and Hi-C fruit drinks, which imply they are a substitute for real juice although they contain only 40 percent as much vitamin C and considerably more H_2O. Even more confusion is caused by diet foods claiming to be low, lower, or lowest in calorie content, without defining their terms or relating them to the full calorie equivalent, a practice the FDA has been unsuccessfully trying to rationalize in its dietary food regulations.

Why—allowing for the inherently rotten streak in human nature —are a persistent minority of the public and the food industry permitted to go on trying to rob each other blind?

Part of the trouble is that our legal system allows one or the other to get away with a little too much. In the case of shoplifting and bad checks (one of the few areas where the public has the edge over the industry) it is almost impossible for stores to prosecute offenders unless they actually catch them in the act or can prove a deliberate attempt to defraud. While this is an extremely valuable safeguard for the innocent, a criminal can often make hay. The 2–10 day waiting period before a merchant or bank can issue a complaint against a bad check is a great advantage for the person who is a bad credit risk or who has made a mistake in the balance in his account. It also enables an astute forger to hit the same store more than once and be states away before the law catches up with him. Another sore point with the industry is that penalties for shoplifting are extremely inconsistent. About half have no specified penalty at all; others range from a $5 fine in West Virginia, to 1–7 years in jail in Oregon.[25]

In most other cases the situation tends to favor industry. Charges of deceptive advertising, particularly in the nutrition field, are often extremely hard to prove. The FTC can take years to build up a case, which the manufacturers will fight through the courts, all the while making money out of the product in question. The drive against the freezer beef racket, for example, is creeping forward on a case-by-case basis. During 1967 the FTC had more than thirty-five investigations under way, eight of which eventually produced judgments against the companies concerned.

Overcome by despair or intertia (it is hard to tell which) the FTC has in recent years concentrated on what a zoologist would call displacement activities. Unable to cope with the larger problems of deception and conglomerate growth, it hounds the small fry—the fraudulent chinchilla breeders and the mislabelers of fur coats. However, a small improvement occurred in 1969 following stinging and well documented exposés by Ralph Nader and his "raiders,"[26] the American Bar Association,[27] and (the unkindest cut of all) from FTC Commissioner Elman at the hearings on regulatory agencies held by the Administrative Practice subcommittee of the Senate Judiciary Committee. Needled by charges of ineptitude and cronyism, the Commission began a new campaign against deceptive advertising. Within a few months it found its first target —the Campbell Soup Co., which was adding clear glass marbles to make its soup look heartier before the TV cameras.[28]

Weights and measures enforcement is extremely uneven. In 1968 only twenty-seven states had adopted the National Conference of Weights and Measures Model Law, which is intended to provide a uniform framework for packaging, and weights and measures inspection procedures. Some of the remaining states have equally good laws of their own, but others have worse ones. Few have the money and inspection staff to do a really efficient job. Some have no control over short-weight merchandise, which is returned to the packer, and in some cases simply finds its way to other outlets or more tolerant parts of the country. Hardly any have established standards of fill. Many state inspectors have no power to issue injunctions which keep erring firms in line, others have no package checking programs, are reluctant to prosecute offenders, and fitful about investigating consumer complaints. To cap it all, a few directorships of weights and measures are political jobs, exposing incumbents to threats of political reprisals and pressure to "go easy."

The public is partly to blame for this. Many people are blissfully unaware that they have a weights and measures bureau at all, let alone prepared to fight on its behalf at their state legislature. Such apathy has opened the way for vested interests to keep inspection down to a bare minimum, either by financial starvation, or by limiting the authority of the weights and measures staff.

This same combination of public apathy and private pressure has helped maintain a legal gray area in which people vaguely believe they are getting more protection than is actually the case. Sad to say, a good deal of so-called consumer protection is primarily designed to help industry sell more, under better competitive conditions, and to maintain public confidence in the end product. The result is an uneasy compromise between what consumers expect and what industry is willing to provide.

One stunted fruit of this compromise is Truth in Packaging. A second is the present law relating to food standards and the way these are formulated. In theory, they are excellent protection for both consumers and reputable manufacturers; in practice, they are criticized by both sides. Industry complains that they hamper product innovation, and clip the wings of anyone wishing to market a superior product. From the public's point of view, they often result in food which is average or poor in quality, at least for anyone who knows what the good home-prepared or gourmet version is like. Worse yet, the ingredients are not listed on the package. Consumers are presumed to know what they are getting—though the ads do not tell them, and only a minute fraction of the population ever bothers to read the Code of Federal Regulations, titles, 7, 9, and 21, where these standards are published.

Part of the trouble is that the federal agencies that work with the food industry do so by negotiation rather than by compulsion, and cannot force a standard which is unacceptably high, particuarly in the absence of strong consumer support. Some do not try very hard. The U.S. Department of Agriculture and the U.S. Department of the Interior (Bureau of Commercial Fisheries) primarily represent the processor rather than the consumer. The USDI is so producer-oriented that fish standards remain voluntary and are used by a small fraction of the industry.

Even the much more consumer-minded FDA labors under a disadvantage. The 1968 budget for foods standards development was a mere $280,000, with a staff of only 18. Since standards can take years to develop, particularly if the FDA does the homework, it is hardly surprising that the agency is nowhere near catching up with existing products, let alone all the new ones that are swamping the marketplace.

The legal process in standard making prevents the FDA from act-ing quickly, yet there are no administrative or financial incentives for consumers to play a regular part in the decision-making.

If industry opposes a standard or disagrees over the details the proceedings can be held up almost indefinitely. During the peanut butter affair, first the Peanut Butter Manufacturers Association, then certain members, disputed the exact ratio of peanuts to oils and sweetener. The FDA pressed for 90 percent peanuts; the industry countered with 87 percent. The FDA first tried for a standard in 1959, then almost every year since. Each time manufacturers complained that the 10 percent limit on oil was too low, that their products would lack spreadability, and, as a clincher, claimed that millions of kids who consume peanut butter so avidly in its present form could not be wrong. At the end of 1969 the FDA was still stymied—this time by an appeal from Skippy and Peter Pan.

Looking at the whole supermarket underworld, with its delicately balanced predatory forces, there is only one person who really benefits—the thief who gets away with it.

Each year food stores lose an estimated 2–5 percent in inventory shrink from all sources,[29] or 2–4 times their net profit. On the basis of approximately $77 billion in retail sales, it comes to a staggering $2.6–$6.6 billion. They lose $240 million more in bad checks. There is also the expense of security precautions—guards, devices, credit information systems—plus the administrative cost of recovering bad checks and lost carts. Not all of this is a dead loss. Stores can obtain insurance against employee theft, burglary, and in some cases, riot damage and vandalism, though this is expensive and becoming increasingly more so. They can also write off the balance as a tax loss (everyone has to pay to make up for the lost tax revenue). Even so, it all adds to the cost of doing business, produces nothing in extra sales, and ultimately goes on the grocery bill.

Customers also pay for stores' and manufacturers' economic offenses, particularly short-weighting. What this particular bill is no one knows. However, intelligent guesses extracted by Dr. Gordon during his surveys run from $5,460,000 a year in Pennsylvania,

$24 million a year in California, to blanket figures of $54 per family to $150 per person annually. What consumers pay for products which have been adulterated, for advertising that is misleading, and food standards which are unintelligible is also anyone's guess, though the price in frustration and disillusion must be substantial.

What can we do to protect ourselves? It goes without saying that we and our children should not steal, remove carts, drop bottles, nibble, or dump unwanted merchandise in awkward places. We should also keep a close watch over our finances to make sure that checks never bounce. If we see a shoplifter in action, a quiet word to the manager is greatly appreciated. No arrest will be made until store personnel actually catch the thief in the act, and there is no danger of an outsider becoming involved. A suspicious person will be closely watched, and probably caught, if not this time then on another shopping trip.

In Pacific Beach, California, a group of women have formed a "Housewives Alert" to combat shoplifting. In the course of their own shopping, members report anyone—customer or employee—they see stealing. The group has had a lot of local publicity, in itself a useful deterrent, and would like the idea copied in other parts of the country.

Shoppers could also use a good deal more vigilance on their own behalf, particularly at the checkout. It is a good idea periodically to checkweigh meat and fresh produce on the store's own scales. It is essential to remember the price you are supposed to be paying for advertised items, and watch the checker like a hawk. If necessary ask her to go more slowly and call out all prices. Request a recheck if you think she has made a mistake, is weighing "on the swing," or the scales do not start at zero. Anyone who has been short-weighted should complain to the store, which will probably give a refund.

If the store is uncooperative, call the local department of weights and measures. If the sealer is worth his salt, he will arrange for a "test shop" in the particular store, to make sure short-weighting is not chronic.[*30] Any shopper whose blood is really up at being cheated, and is prepared to take some time and trouble, can also sue the offending store in the small claims court, or (depending on local regulations) even ask about the possibility of bringing a class action on behalf of other shoppers in the same predicament.*[31] The value of such tactics is not, of course, the money, but the publicity that can result, assuming that the shopper takes the trouble to contact the local press.

While consumers can do little about the competitive climate that results in short-weighting, misrepresenting, or tampering with the product, they could achieve much more than they do now by taking a more active political interest in what the regulatory agencies are doing, particularly the FDA, and their state departments of weights and measures. The FDA is always crying for consumer evidence on the need for food standards, but, with honorable exceptions like the Federation of Homemakers of Arlington, Virginia, who fought so valiantly for better peanut butter, they rarely get enough of it. Another way consumers can be effective is to exert some influence on their state legislatures by supporting good legislation, writing letters, attending hearings if possible, urging that weights and measures budgets be increased, and generally nagging legislators to get something useful done.

Eight

SHOPPING PROBLEMS OF THE POOR

The manager of that grocery store must think we are a bunch of animals. The floors are filthy, there are flies all over the place, they handle our food with dirty hands and never say thank you or anything that's nice.

A WATTS RESIDENT
After the 1965 riots

While most of us are occasional victims of the supermarket under-world, there are millions of people today who run a still graver risk of being cheated when they go food shopping. They are the poor and the elderly, and particularly the elderly poor, who spend more for food and get less value for their money than their affluent neigh-bors. They are the exceptions to the industry's boast that we are the best fed nation in the world and spend a smaller propor-tion of our income on food than other countries. They are the vic-tims of the seediest and least efficient end of the free enterprise system, which penalizes them for being poor and trapped, and from which they find it hard to escape. They are victims of a democratic system which has made 90 percent of its people rich by repressing the 10 percent at the bottom of the heap, and which allows farmers to produce more food than they can sell while thousands of people to go to bed hungry every night.

Today there are 25.4 million people living at or below poverty level, earning less than $3,553 for an urban family of four. This includes 9 million on welfare, and another 7 million over 65 who have incomes of less than $1,800 a year. And they spend some 40 percent of their take-home money on food, compared to the national average of 16.8 percent.[1] Slightly more than half of them live in big cities like New York, Chicago, Los Angeles, Philadelphia, and Detroit.

Not only do they spend proportionately more for food, they pay higher prices for it. There are very few supermarkets in the urban ghettos where some 15 million of the poor live, probably not many more than 1,000 in the entire country. Unlike suburban shoppers, who have a choice of five or six supermarkets within easy reach, ghetto residents are lucky if they can find one.

It is clear that the free enterprise system, which is so eager to serve the prosperous suburbs, whimpers to a halt at the edge of the ghetto. Many food chains find that operating costs there are 2–3 percent higher—more than enough to wipe out their annual profit.[2] Occupancy costs (rent, equipment, insurance, and utilities) run 5 percent of sales instead of the usual 4 percent because the volume of business against which they are measured is low. Labor costs are 10 percent as compared to 9, because of the problems of staff training and recruiting, resulting in poor productivity. Gross profit is 1 percent lower, owing to higher pilferage and lower sales of high-margin specialty foods.

Adding to these woes are the difficulty and discomfort of doing business in the ghetto. Land is hard to obtain, particularly in the 40,000–80,000 sq. ft. lots which large supermarkets need. Premises tend to be cramped and old-fashioned. Staff are hard to find, train, and keep, and the threat of ghetto violence—holdups, muggings, tire slashings—erodes the morale of those who do stick it out.

Lacking chain supermarkets within walking distance, or transportation to the suburbs, the poor patronize the "mom and pop" stores which used to dominate the grocery scene. Unfortunately they are more expensive than either the supermarkets or the affiliated independents. A special six-city study by the Bureau of Labor Statistics during 1966 showed that they charged 2½ percent more than their competitors.[3] Other studies suggest that the discrepancy may be even greater. In Watts[4] they charge 7–10 percent more than food stores in the rest of the city; in Philadelphia, 16 percent more, in Detroit, 20 percent more, and in Fort Wayne, Ind., 27 percent more.[5] It has been estimated that ghetto residents could save up to 20 percent of their food bill if reputable chains would move into their area.[6]

Mom and pop are not necessarily gouging, though to their patrons it may look that way. They experience all the difficult business conditions of chain store operators, aggravated by their smallness and lack of financial resources. Their turnover rate is extremely low, their insurance more costly. They cannot buy in bulk, get favorable discounts, or subsidize their flagging profits from fatter suburban outlets. As a result, they can offer fewer specials, and only stay in business by charging higher prices.

The typical ghetto market is a far cry from the bright, amply stocked, and well-serviced suburban emporium. A witness before the National Commission on Food Marketing said: "You will usually find congested aisles, overcrowded meat and vegetable counters, fewer choices of any items, a questionable quality of produce especially, and many items without prices on them."[7] Surveys made all over the country bear this out,[8] and show poor physical conditions, lower grade meat, and wilted produce bought in the "late" wholesale market. There are also fewer promotions, and when the jackpot prizes for supermarket games are handed out, they are planted among prosperous suburban matrons rather than their ghetto counterparts.

The stores' troubles are caused in part by sloppy merchandising and inadequate refrigeration, and by a lower turnover, which leaves perishable merchandise to spoil on the shelves. These dingy symptoms all point to the breakdown of competition, which is normally vigorous enough to keep suburban stores on their toes. More disturbing—and alien to the food industry's emphasis on good customer relations—is a tendency to harass the ghetto shopper which would not be tolerated elsewhere. While some stores (mostly mom and pop) offer credit and call you by your name, others will not cash personal checks, or demand so much proof of identification that the customer is embarrassed.*⁹ Others carry warning signs against shoplifting, conspicuously placed mirrors, and even employ an armed guard, making it clear that the management does not trust its patrons. Rainchecks against out-of-stock specials are often not given, or not implemented, and complaints are handled with scant courtesy, that is, when the poor can nerve themselves to complain.

To be fair to ghetto merchants, the poor are not the most desirable customers. They spend less, they can often only afford to buy one meal at a time, they take less advantage of specials (and are not as likely to be drawn in to the store to make impulse purchases), and they are forced to make do with cheaper cuts of meat. On welfare, they tend to splurge twice a month when the relief checks come, and not buy much in between.

The poor are more easily deceived than the suburban shopper. Many are handicapped by age and education. It is difficult to read the entire label if you are functionally illiterate, if you do not understand English too well, or if your eyesight simply will not take in small print. For the same reasons, food grades and standards, and stores' cherished device of multiple pricing are too confusing to work out. The children often do the shopping, particularly when the mothers work, and they are more easily fooled over prices and quality.

Even their choice of foods works against them. In aggregate they spend millions of dollars more than they need to by buying the national brands seen on TV in preference to the cheaper store brand equivalents. Anthony Spaeth, president of Controlled Brand Marketing, which surveyed the subject in 1969, explained, "Lacking the confidence that education provides and wary of being exploited, the poor seek the reassurance of quality that national brands provide, as well as vicarious participation in the American way of life portrayed in advertising."*10

They are even penalized when they buy ethnic specialties. The "soul food" liked by many Negro families—which accounts for as much as 25 percent of grocery sales in ghetto areas—often carry colossal margins. Greens, for instance, carry margins of 34.2–60.5 percent, compared to the produce department average of 30.1 percent, while chitlins and other specialties have a margin anywhere up to two and a half times the meat department average.

Elderly people have additional problems which make it hard for many of them to get full value for their money, quite apart from poverty. Malnutrition or obesity are widespread. Many people are sold on diet foods and vitamin supplements, which they may not be able to afford and which may not do them much good. Many rely heavily on convenience foods, particularly TV dinners.[11] Though these dinners are much better than tea and toast if you live alone and have lost all heart to cook, they are more expensive and generally poorer in food value than home prepared meals. Nearly all older people would like to buy foods in small quantities, which are hard to find in these days of family sizes.

Caught in the vicious circle of poverty, the poor and the stores which serve them are trapped by the worst aspects of the free enterprise system. And it is likely that the poor are also at the receiving end of a greater amount of deliberate fraud and price discrimination than the suburban middle class.

Short-weighting, a serious enough problem nationally, seems more widespread in low-income areas. According to Leland Gordon's surveys, mom and pop stores were the commonest type of market found guilty of repeated short-weighting. A survey in New York found that 12 percent of the scales in the sample were inaccurate.[12] One was off more than 50 percent in calculating the price of chickens, which were being sold at $1.53 instead of the market price of 97¢ (none of the customers protested). Similar results were found by the New York Department of Markets when a team of low-income shoppers turned their purchases over to a weights and measures inspector for on-the-spot checking.[13]

Another criticism is fraudulent or misleading advertising by food stores. In the New York study "less than 20 percent of the ads surveyed . . . contained more than 10 items per week which showed any reduction in price."[14] Another study, which surveyed three A & P markets in East Harlem, found that "at least 20 items in each store were either higher priced than advertised or unavailable altogether."

Coupled with this are a number of sloppy merchandising practices of which all food chains are guilty, particularly in low-income areas. In its study of two cities,[15] the FTC found that in the Washington, D.C. ghetto 23 percent of specials were unobtainable vs. 11 percent in the suburbs, while in San Francisco the respective rates were 7 and 5 percent. Also, between 5 and 10 percent of the regular shelf prices were incorrectly marked, half the time too high.

A more serious complaint is that certain supermarket chains charge higher prices for some foods in low-income areas. Evidence from university professors, newspapers, anti-poverty, women's, and political groups has mounted in recent years, culminating in a blast from eight different organizations before a subcommittee of the House Committee on Government Operations in the fall of 1967.[16] A related charge is that some ghetto stores raise prices on "mother's day," the 1st and 15th of the month, when the welfare checks are cashed.

The shifting nature of food prices makes these points difficult to prove, particularly since three seemingly authoritative federal surveys failed to find any such price discrimination.[17] And, naturally, the food industry is loud in its denial that either practice exists.

In reply to critics, Clarence G. Adamy, president of the National Association of Food Chains, said that prices are set according to a series of zones, each centering on the chain's warehouse, and are based on the transportation costs and advertising media reach. Prices are uniform within each area, allowing for local managers' discretion to lower them to meet competition or move surplus stocks. Any discrepancies which occur are due to human error. It would be bad business and cost too much in wages to scurry around and alter prices when the welfare checks are cashed.

It is notable that citizens' groups and the newspapers found evidence of price discrimination, while business and the government did not.[18] One explanation may be that all three federal surveys were preceded by a blast of publicity which was sufficiently loud to warn food chains that they would be surveyed, while private groups were not only anonymous but unannounced. Even so, the line-up of all these findings is so neat that one suspects that each party discovered precisely what it was or was not looking for.

Sifting the mass of contradictory evidence, it appears that although some of the anti-poverty and other amateur groups made a few mistakes in their surveys, they still found a core of disquieting evidence which not even the government studies can explain.*[19]

A few merchants in Watts, Cincinnati, and St. Louis have admitted to the press that they jack up prices to meet difficult business conditions in the ghetto.[20] Two grocery groups told the House *Hearings* that they had lately expelled member stores for not sticking to advertised prices.[21] And grocers in the Mississippi Delta told the *Wall Street Journal* that they raised prices when food stamps were introduced.

The chains are probably right in saying that most price differences are the result of human error. Supermarkets are caught in the price-juggling trap they themselves invented. The gargantuan task of changing thousands of prices each week is often tackled by part-time, high school, or student help, who do not always do a thorough job. This adds to the error rate by checkers, who either guess the price if not marked, or ring up the higher of two or three different prices.

Management problems are also involved. The FTC concluded[22] that there was a need for "additional controls over low-income area stores, including more frequent price and inventory checks, stronger supervision at the district level, and changes in the manner in which store managers are assigned and compensated. At present, it appears that the least efficient managers often are assigned to low-income area stores. These managers may be tempted to cut corners to improve their stores' performance." However reasonable these explanations may be, many of the poor (who tend not to read government reports) still feel they are being cheated.

A tragic expression of their bitterness is the large number of food stores looted, burned, or totally destroyed in recent years, particularly during the 1965–1967 riots. While part of the damage was caused by indiscriminate mob violence, a good deal was due to simple revenge, in which food and other stores were primary targets. The casualty list is staggering: in Detroit, at least 75 supermarkets (15 percent of the city total) and 75–125 small grocery stores were destroyed or damaged; in Cleveland, 25 supermarkets were looted or burned, to the tune of $1 million in damages; and Watts lost 21 grocery stores of all kinds. After the assassination of Dr. Martin Luther King, 50 grocery stores in Washington were blitzed, including 19 Safeways, the chain which had been specifically accused of price gouging the year before.

Unfortunately for the ghettos, this instant urban renewal has only served to downgrade the already inferior food distribution system by smashing many of the supermarkets which *did* operate there. Each major outbreak of violence has produced high prices and a scarcity of food, followed by canceled insurance policies or increased premiums for damaged or destroyed stores, many of which have closed for good and have not been replaced.

During the past two or three years there has been increasing pressure from informed public opinion, and consumer-minded legislators and federal officials to make the food industry assume more social responsibility for providing the poor with a reliable low-cost food supply. On all sides the chains are being urged to set up shop in the ghetto on a bigger scale. Food manufacturers, too, are being accused of producing enriched, high-protein foods for the poor overseas while neglecting the needy on their own doorstep.

Industry's very limited response to these urgings illustrates the fact that in our capitalist society the giant food firms are not set up to embark on many projects which will be long-term losers, or, rather, they are highly selective about which these losing projects shall be. Ironically for the poor, manufacturers will risk a good deal of money on new products which frequently flop, rather than specially enriched basic foodstuffs which might break even but will never hit the jackpot. Chains, too, will subsidize some un-profitable stores—but seldom in the ghetto, where they will never make fat profits.

Only a few chains are expanding in or entering low-income areas, notably A & P, which has the reputation of being willing to open stores *anywhere*. Others are concentrating on the valuable but subsidiary task of recruiting and training black employees, or experimenting with projects which bring the maximum of good-will with the minimum of investment. Safeway, for example, has been supplying free management know-how to the faltering (black) Hunters Point Co-op in San Francisco, and offering a limited number of staple products on "special" in its Washington, D.C., sales area around the first of the month when the welfare checks are cashed.

A similar situation prevails at the manufacturing end. Only a minority of companies are undertaking substantial nutrition re-search, or marketing specially enriched products. There is no ques-tion that they have the know-how to fortify *anything*. Unfortu-nately, they fear that it will not pay off, or that they will incur huge expenses for promoting unfamiliar new products.

Recently some manufacturers have admitted the urgent need for fortification, at least of staple products. But unless we are careful, the consumer payoff could be undesirable. Along with the re-moval of genuine legal barriers, mostly existing food standards, industry would like the abolition of inconvenient marketing re-strictions which nonetheless protect shoppers of all incomes.

While waiting for the giants to act, non-violent, ambitious stir-